Kant's Rational Theology

ALLEN W. WOOD is Associate Professor of Philosophy at Cornell University. A graduate of Reed College, he received his M.A. and Ph.D. degrees from Yale University.

By the same author

Kant's Moral Religion

Immanuel Kant, *Lectures on Philosophical Theology*, translated with Gertrude M. Clark

KANT'S
Rational Theology

Allen W. Wood

Cornell University Press
Ithaca and London

THIS BOOK HAS BEEN PUBLISHED WITH THE AID OF A GRANT FROM THE HULL
MEMORIAL PUBLICATION FUND OF CORNELL UNIVERSITY.

First published 1978 by Cornell University Press.
Published in the United Kingdom by Cornell University Press Ltd.,
2-4 Brook Street, London W1Y 1AA.

International Standard Book Number 0-8014-1200-5
Library of Congress Catalog Card Number 78-58059
Printed in the United States of America
*Librarians: Library of Congress cataloging information
appears on the last page of the book.*

To my parents,
Forrest and Alleen Wood

Contents

Preface

This book was conceived while I was working on a translation
of Immanuel Kant's *Lectures on Philosophical Theology*. It began as
a critical essay to be included in that volume, an essay of the sort
that translators commonly inflict on the reader as their price for
undertaking the important but thankless task of making a valu-
able piece of writing available to those who cannot read it or
haven't the time to struggle through it in the original language.
But in the course of its composition, the critical essay grew into
a little book in its own right, which it now seems best to publish
separately.

Kant's thinking about theology, and about religious subjects
generally, has two distinct aspects: one practical or moral, the
other theoretical or metaphysical. It is clear that for Kant himself
the moral side of religious questions is by far the most important
one, and he takes the moral standpoint on the question of God's
existence and on other theological issues to be the only one capable of yielding any positive results. But Kant's metaphysical
or theoretical reflections are of interest on account of their originality and intrinsic philosophical merit, their historical influence, and the light they shed on the tradition of rational theology in medieval and modern philosophy. This aspect of Kant's
philosophy is also of importance for an understanding of his
thought as a whole, and specifically for a proper appreciation of
the contents of Kantian moral faith.

In my book *Kant's Moral Religion*, I dealt almost exclusively with the practical or moral side of Kant's thought about religious issues. But as I worked through Kant's philosophy from this point of view, I could not help being aware that the specific religious conclusions Kant expects the morally disposed man to draw from his predicament are very much a part of a long tradition of metaphysics and rational theology, a tradition on which Kant no doubt turns a critical eye, but to which, in the end, he belongs every bit as much as the metaphysicians he criticizes. The contents of Kantian moral faith turn out to depend very heavily on the outcome of Kant's theoretical investigations in the area of rational theology, even though this outcome, considered in itself, is extremely cautious, tentative, and skeptical. We cannot, I realized, have a full or balanced understanding of Kant's thought on religious subjects so long as we fail to take account of his reflections, often exceedingly abstract, obscure, and subtle, concerning the rational origin, content, and status of our concept of a supreme being. Consequently, it seemed to me very natural to complement my earlier book on Kant's moral religion with a study of his rational theology.

The topic of this book is, in any case, hardly one that has been overworked in the scholarly literature. A good deal of attention, it is true, has been devoted to Kant's famous attacks on the three brands of theistic proof. Even so, it seems to me that there is widespread misunderstanding of Kant's ideas in this area on several points, and (as I argue) the philosophical force of Kant's critique of these proofs has often been greatly overestimated. With regard to the positive or constructive aspects of Kant's rational theology, however, the very reverse is true. Few writers have even condescended to discuss the opening sections of the Ideal of Pure Reason or made any attempt to explicate sympathetically the difficult line of reasoning that is so tersely and obscurely expressed in this despised and neglected portion of the *Critique of Pure Reason*. The only book-length treatment of Kant's rational theology in English, F. E. England's *Kant's Conception of God*, was written in 1929, and from a standpoint that is not particularly sympathetic either to Kant himself or to any contemporary philosophers who might be interested in what he had to say on the subject of philosophical theology. The fact that

England's book was reprinted not many years ago leads me to believe that there is a need for an English study on this aspect of Kant's philosophy. The present book is intended to help fill that need.

On some points in this book I was aided by discussions with other philosophers, and in particular with Kenneth Nelson, Carl Ginet, and Robert Stalnaker. None of them has read any portion of the manuscript, however, and they might not recognize their contributions to it if they saw them. I want also to thank my wife, Rega, as always, for her continuing support of all my work, and my son, Henry, for waiting to be born until I got this book finished.

ALLEN W. WOOD

Ithaca, New York

Kant's Rational Theology

Introduction

Kant is not usually thought of as a theologian. He is, in fact, remembered principally as a critic of the tradition of natural theology, on account of his influential attacks on the received proofs for God's existence. The common conception of his relationship to tradition was perhaps articulated most forcefully by Heinrich Heine, who portrayed Kant as a kind of theological Robespierre, a soulless, ruthless, and incorruptible executioner of the Deity. Of course, Kant does claim to be denying knowledge only to make room for faith; and in Heine's myth too Kant is depicted as relenting at the last, for the sake of his old servant Lampe, and permitting God to exist at least for the eyes of morality. But Kant's attempt to undo in his practical philosophy the work of destruction accomplished in the *Critique of Pure Reason* was viewed by Heine, and by most of Kant's subsequent readers, as both less successful and less characteristically Kantian than his theoretical undermining of the metaphysical basis of traditional theism.[1]

Heine's fantasy does contain an important element of truth. As an ardent supporter of the Enlightenment, Kant does not hesitate to express his mistrust of clericalism and traditional

1. Heinrich Heine, *Religion und Philosophie in Deutschland, Gesammelte Werke,* ed. Gustav Karpeles (Berlin, 1887), 5:95ff. Cf. *Religion and Philosophy in Germany,* trans. John Snodgrass (Boston, 1959), pp. 105ff. All translations from German, French, and Latin are my own. Standard English translations are also cited for the convenience of the reader.

ecclesiastical institutions. He is the bitter opponent of any faith which encourages contempt for human reason and seeks to deprive it of its rightful sovereignty over thought and action. The only really acceptable religion for Kant is a religion of pure reason. He himself has only contempt for creeds whose main appeal is to our morbid emotions and for systems of "fanaticism" (*Schwärmerei*) which found themselves on extravagant aspirations to mystical theosophy. Kant is willing to condone a faith which bases itself on special divine revelation only insofar as the content of its revelation accords with the precepts revealed naturally to every human being through the faculty of reason. And of course it was on account of Kant's repeated and open attacks on the "superstitious pseudo-service of God" in contemporary religious institutions that the Prussian minister Johann Christoph Wöllner finally forbade him to write on matters pertaining to religion.

In the area of natural theology too Kant is a profound critic of the tradition of scholastic rationalism and its claims to natural knowledge about God. In the Analytic of the first critique, Kant argues that the human faculty of knowledge is limited to the world of sense; and in the Dialectic of the same work, he systematically criticizes the attempts of rationalist metaphysics to overcome this limitation. Kant's immediate target, of course, is the rationalism of eighteenth-century Germans such as Christian Wolff and Alexander Gottlieb Baumgarten. But in a broader sense, the tradition he attacks is one which goes back many centuries. In it, the religious ideas derived from Hebrew monotheism found expression and defense in a metaphysics derived from the Greeks. This tradition, moreover, not only survived but actually drew strength from the modern scientific revolution. (In this connection, it should not be forgotten that the three principal theistic arguments, as Kant knew them, were closely associated with the names of Descartes, Leibniz, and Newton.) It is certainly understandable that Kant's attack on traditional theology should have been experienced by his contemporaries, and even a half century later by Heine, as something profoundly disturbing. In this sense, perhaps, it really was no exaggeration for Heine to speak of Kant as the *Weltzermalmender*, "the great destroyer in the kingdom of thought."[2]

At the same time, however, Heine's account entirely overlooks Kant's profound sympathy with the tradition he criticized. Kant does reject its arguments for God's existence, and turns something of a skeptical eye on its claims to speculative knowledge of the divine nature. But in the end, Kant is fundamentally unable to conceive of the human situation except theistically, and unable to conceive of God in any terms except those of the scholastic-rationalist tradition. Kant's criticism of the tradition is not intended by the philosopher himself to crush its intellectual world, or to destroy its kingdom of thoughts. Kant no more considered wandering outside its intellectual world than he did of leaving the vicinity of his native Königsberg. And his philosophy, viewed integrally and as a whole, actually leaves the traditional kingdom of thought pretty much intact. For Kant's real aim is not to destroy theology, but to replace a dogmatic theology with a critical one: to transform rational theology from a complacent speculative science into a critical examination of the inevitable but perpetually insoluble problems of human reason, and a vehicle for the expression of our moral aspirations under the guidance of an autonomous reason.

Theology and the Natural Dialectic of Reason

For Kant, the pseudosciences of rationalist metaphysics all have their foundation in a natural tendency of human reason to transcend its limits and to seek a completeness in its knowledge which it will be forever beyond the finite nature of humanity to achieve. The occasion for these vain but inevitable inquiries is provided by what Kant calls the "ideas of reason." The term *idea* is borrowed by Kant quite consciously from Plato.[3] It refers to any of several concepts formed a priori by our rational faculty, to which no possible experience can correspond. An idea of reason interests us because it appears to give our knowledge a

2. Heine, *Werke*, 5:98. Cf. *Religion and Philosophy in Germany*, p. 109.
3. Kant, *Critique of Pure Reason*, A 313/B 370; *Gesammelte Schriften*, Berlin Academy Edition, vols. 3 and 4.

certain "completeness" by providing the "unconditioned" in relation to a set or a series of objects which are given in our experience as "conditioned" in a certain way.

The Dialectic of the *Critique of Pure Reason* presents a whole system of such ideas, and it attempts systematically to refute the pretended claims to knowledge associated with them. The pseudoscience of rational psychology is based on the idea of a simple, indestructible (and hence immortal) soul-substratum which is supposed to underlie all my thoughts and inner experiences as the substance in which they inhere, and as the explanatory ground for their a priori necessary unity and coherence. This idea represents to us the "unconditioned" in relation to the various mutually limiting and conditioned phenomena of my inner conscious life. Or again, the pretended science of pure rational cosmology takes as its theme the ideas of unconditioned completeness in relation to various regressive series given in our experience. It focuses on the idea of a necessarily first moment in time, or a necessarily indivisible substance, as the "unconditioned" in relation to the temporally conditioned series of events, or the series of (possible) sets of division of which a given corporeal substance is susceptible. On the Kantian theories of self-awareness, of space and time, and of material substance, none of these ideas represents an object to which any possible experience can ever correspond. And thus on Kant's epistemology, all the attempts of rational psychology and rational cosmology to inquire after the properties of such objects, or even to establish their existence (or nonexistence) must be abandoned as hopeless.

Alongside the pseudosciences of rational psychology and rational cosmology, Kant treated also the pretensions of rational theology to provide us with a priori knowledge of the existence and attributes of a supreme being. Roughly stated, the idea of a necessary being, according to Kant, arises in the course of rational cosmology, when we attempt to think the "unconditioned" in respect to a series of things whose existence is causally contingent each upon the next. But the most proper idea of God, as a supremely perfect being or *ens realissimum*, is constructed by our reason in quite a different way: it comes about in the course of our attempt to conceive the conditions for the "thorough determination" of things, that is, the unconditionally complete knowledge of them, or the thoroughgoing specification of all the properties belonging to them. Again roughly stated, Kant's theory is that since the idea of a most perfect being includes in it every possible perfection or reality, the complete set of properties which might belong to any possible thing could (in theory) be determined by limiting or selecting from the properties of God in the right way. The idea of God therefore provides us with a (purely abstract) conception of "the material of all possibility," of a source from which all the properties of any and every possible thing could in principle be derived. Of course, our finite reason has no access to any such source in the concrete, and our determination of the properties of things must proceed by the gradual accumulation of empirical knowledge, which will always fall far short of completeness. Yet we can be distinctly aware of our finitude in this respect only insofar as we have the capacity to form some conception (however vague and inadequate) of what the completion of our task might be like. Thus we quite naturally come upon the idea of a supreme being, in Kant's view, a being whose properties, if we could know them concretely, would enable us to accomplish a thorough determination of any other possible thing.

The idea of God is a necessary idea of reason, and Kant has only respect for our natural interest in the content of this idea and our theoretical curiosity about the existence or nonexistence of an object corresponding to it. As we can see from his *Lectures on Philosophical Theology*, he enters quite sympathetically into the traditional inquiries of rational theology. He even thinks that a certain amount can be known about the content of the idea of God and the attributes which must be thought in it, although on closer examination nearly all this knowledge turns out to be of a purely "negative" nature—a knowledge of the respects in which the various qualities of finite, sensible (and therefore to us properly knowable) things cannot be correctly ascribed to an *ens realissimum*. Kant's only real quarrel is with those who pretend to transform theology from a necessary object of theoretical curiosity into a speculative science, a body of demonstrated doctrine about God. For not only does Kant think that such knowledge is not accessible to us, but he also believes that from a moral point of view it would be a basic falsification of the human predicament to suppose that it could be obtained.

Moral Faith

In the second edition of the *Critique of Pure Reason*, Kant wrote: "Thus I must deny *knowledge* in order to find a place for *faith*; for the dogmatism of metaphysics, that is, the prejudice that it is possible to make progress in metaphysics without a criticism of pure reason, is the true source of that unbelief, always very dogmatic, which conflicts with morality."[4] The real shallowness of Heine's picture shows itself in the fact that he treats this idea as an afterthought, a half-hearted concession to religious orthodoxy, or to the sentimentalism of those who (like old Lampe, or, indeed like Heine himself, at least at this point in his intellectual career) are unable to muster the coldness of spirit necessary to accept a godless universe. The truth is rather that an attitude of rational religious faith lies at the foundation of the critical philosophy, and of its vision of man as a finite rational being who has moral autonomy as his proper destination.

The dignity of a rational being, according to Kant, consists in the fact that such a being is an autonomous agent, a spontaneous source of the rational laws which define his own destination. The supreme good for man, in other words, does not consist in bringing himself into harmony with an order (natural, social, or supernatural) given outside him, but rather in generating his own system of order and imposing it freely on his own actions and on the world. At the same time, however, human nature is finite, subjected to a natural world which it may to some degree know, and which is open in part to the effects of its rational choice. It is in this world that the human agent must try to realize the purposes set by his autonomous reason. To be sure, his ability to choose autonomously does not depend on the course of nature. But the fate of his moral projects and purposes, to which only an attitude of hypocrisy could render him indiffer-

4. *Critique of Pure Reason*, B xxx.

ent, does depend in large part on the ways of the world outside his control. The moral agent therefore must concern himself with the question whether the course of nature ultimately harmonizes or conflicts with his moral purposes. For if there is no such harmony, then the rational man's moral concerns are empty, and his best efforts are destined to fall stillborn into an absurd and irrational world. Of course the supposition of an amoral world order would not do away with our inner awareness of the moral law. But it would render irrational our purposive action in accordance with that law. As Kant puts it, if I did not believe in an ultimate harmony between morality and nature, "I would have to deny my own nature and its eternal moral laws. I would have to cease being a rational man."[5]

It may not be apparent that any such extreme conclusion as this can be justified. But to see why Kant believes that it can, we must take note of certain conditions which Kant thinks necessary for rational purposive action to be possible. Kant holds that a person can rationally act in pursuit of a given end only so long as he believes that this end is possible of attainment through the course of action he is taking. Suppose, for instance, that someone teaches me a very complicated and difficult game of solitaire. I master the rules and play the game a few times, losing each time. Slightly irritated by this and thirsting for victory, I continue to play the game, fifty times, a hundred times, continuing to lose every time. At last the person who taught me the game takes pity on my frustration and reveals that he has been playing a joke on me. He explains that the game is so constructed that it cannot be won, and he proceeds to demonstrate this sad fact to me. Now as long as I did not realize that the game cannot be won, it still made sense for me to continue trying to win, because I still held the belief (unfortunately false) that if I continued playing the game I might eventually win it. But once I have been persuaded that the game cannot be won, it no longer makes sense for me to keep playing, or at least to keep playing with the aim of winning. To do this would be irrational, if not downright impossible. In general, Kant maintains, I cannot ra-

5. *Gesammelte Schriften*, 28, 2, 2, p. 1072; *Lectures on Philosophical Theology*, trans. Allen W. Wood and Gertrude M. Clark (Ithaca, N.Y., 1978), p. 110.

tionally go on pursuing an aim unless I hold the belief that my aim is at least possible of attainment through the actions I am taking in pursuit of it.

In his argument for moral faith, Kant simply turns this point around. For he holds that the moral law specifies to us a final end or *summum bonum* which our rational nature requires us to pursue. Yet certain elements of this end (such as the apportionment of happiness among rational beings in accordance with their moral deserts) can only be possible of attainment if the course of nature is in ultimate harmony with moral reason. Thus when I act as morality bids me and pursue the highest good, I rationally commit myself to a belief in this harmony.

From a theoretical point of view, of course, this belief is something wholly gratuitous. It is impossible (according to Kant) ever to confirm (or disconfirm) it by any empirical evidence or speculative proof. Only a metaphysical dogmatism (which, as Kant says, is always the source of that unbelief which conflicts with morality) could pretend to show that our final moral purpose is impossible of attainment. Yet Kant also maintains (as we shall see presently) that morality is threatened by dogmatic pretensions in the opposite direction. Morality, therefore, requires that our belief in the attainability of the highest good should not be *knowledge* but *faith*.

Faith and Theology

Kant quite reasonably expresses this moral faith in terms of the pure rational idea of God, and the traditional conception of God's providential care for the world. If the order of nature is the creation of a supremely perfect being, then we can easily conceive how this order accords with our moral end, and how it will ultimately bring to fulfillment the purposes we undertake in pursuit of it. Rational theology, therefore, is not merely an object of theoretical curiosity; it is also an object of deep practical concern, since it is in terms of the idea of God and his relation to the world that we form a clear conception of the content of moral faith.

In the *Lectures on Philosophical Theology*, Kant strongly suggests that if it were not for our moral interest in the concept of

God, there would be no legitimate reason for us to form anything but a "deistic" concept of the supreme being—no reason,
that is, for us to include such "cosmological" predicates as
understanding and volition among its attributes. For only a "living" God, he said, can make a suitable moral impression on us.[6]
Yet it is also important from the moral (as well as the theoretical)
standpoint that rational theology should be pursued *critically*.
Even God's cosmological attributes must be "purified" of empirical limitations before they can be applied to the *ens realissimum*. Kant fears that if we anthropomorphically confuse God's
attributes with the imperfect qualities we meet with empirically
in human beings, our moral vision may be distorted in various
ways. If, for instance, we superstitiously represent moral laws
as arbitrary commands of God like those of a capricious despot
ordering about his servile subjects, then of course we will undermine the very foundations of a morality based on the autonomy of reason. There is, in Kant's view, some such danger
present whenever we permit ourselves to ascribe any of the
qualities of finite beings to God. A careless or dogmatic theology, therefore, which confuses God with the (always merely
sensible and therefore finite) objects accessible to our mode of
cognition is not only guilty of theoretical presumption; it also
threatens to have a corrupting influence on our moral character.

Kant frequently makes the point that his position of skepticism concerning speculative knowledge of God's existence and
attributes has the advantage of protecting faith against those
who would undermine it by pretending to disprove God's existence, or to demonstrate various morally unacceptable conclusions about his nature and operations. But in the *Lectures on
Philosophical Theology*, Kant even goes so far as to claim that the
interest of morality requires skepticism in the other direction as
well. Our belief in God, in order to satisfy the interests of morality, *must* take the form of faith, and *not* of theoretical knowledge:

Hence our faith is not scientific knowledge, and thank heaven it is not!
For God's wisdom is apparent in the very fact that we do not *know* that

6. *Gesammelte Schriften*, 28, 2, 2, pp. 1001f; *Lectures on Philosophical Theology*,
p. 30.

God exists, but should *believe* that God exists. For suppose we could attain to scientific knowledge of God's existence. . . . Then, in this case, all our morality would break down. In his every action, man would represent God to himself as a rewarder or avenger. This image would force itself involuntarily on his soul, and his hope for reward and fear of punishment would take the place of moral motives. Man would be virtuous out of sensuous impulses.[7]

According to Kant, we believe in God because this belief harmonizes with, and is rationally required by, our moral disposition to pursue the highest good. It is because we are morally disposed that we hope our best efforts will be justly rewarded. So long as this hope is a matter of faith and not a matter of knowledge, it cannot undermine our moral conduct by serving as its motive. This is because moral faith presupposes that it is our moral disposition which moves us to believe, and not our knowledge that there is a rewarding and avenging God which disposes us to do what morality commands.

But Kant is not entitled to conclude from these considerations (as he seems to do here) that our moral motivation would necessarily be undermined if we could obtain theoretical knowledge of God's existence. For Kant is in general willing to acknowledge that morally good deeds can sometimes contribute to the happiness of the agent who performs them, and that the agent can sometimes even foresee that this will be the case. In such situations Kant always insists that we can and should be moved by moral considerations and not by the selfish ones which might also move us. But then even if we always knew for certain that our good actions would eventually be rewarded and our evil ones punished (so that morality and prudence, rightly weighed, would always dictate the same course of action), we still should be able to abstract from selfish considerations as far as our motivation is concerned. The most, therefore, that Kant might be entitled to conclude is that the objective uncertainty of our predicament makes moral choice more poignant than it would be if we knew in advance that the right course of action would always necessarily coincide with the self-interested one.

7. *Gesammelte Schriften*, 28, 2, 2, pp. 1083f; *Lectures on Philosophical Theology*, p. 123.

1. The Idea of God

In Kant's view, the rational idea of God has a twofold interest for us: on the one hand, it is the focus of a natural and inevitable (though necessarily fruitless) theoretical inquiry; on the other, it is an object of the highest practical (moral) concern. Of course, there can be no doubt that for Kant the latter interest takes precedence over the former: "What interest does reason have in [theological] knowledge? Not a speculative, but a practical one. . . . Our morality has need of the idea of God to give it emphasis."[1] Yet even Kant's moral theism is in a way dependent on the theoretical idea of God, as it is developed in the *Lectures on Philosophical Theology* and in the Dialectic of the *Critique of Pure Reason*. Kant's argument for moral faith indicates that the morally disposed individual must look upon the highest good as attainable, and on the world of his action as purposively ordered in such a way as to render its attainment possible. But the question may be raised why this moral conviction must take the form of a belief in an extramundane and personal Deity. More recent attempts to express a similar moral or existential vision have not wedded themselves to orthodox theism in the way Kant's did. Fichte's concept of moral faith, in many ways modeled directly on its Kantian precursor, did not follow Kant on this point. Like Kant, Fichte held that the morally disposed individual is rationally committed to believe that the world in which we act (or its

1. *Gesammelte Schriften*, 28, 2, 2, p. 996; *Lectures on Philosophical Theology*, trans. Allen W. Wood and Gertrude M. Clark (Ithaca, N.Y., 1978), p. 24.

supersensible correlate) is in some kind of ultimate conformity with our moral aims. But Fichte saw no need to posit a personal God over and above this impersonal rational order in the moral world. "The living and operative moral order," he declared, "is itself God. We need no other God, and we cannot comprehend any other."[2] A much more recent analogue to Kantian moral faith may be found in Paul Tillich's conception of the "absolute faith" through which man finds the "courage to be" in the face of anxiety and absurdity. Here again, however, orthodox theism has been abandoned in favor of some pantheistic immanence-transcendence, a conception whose very vagueness renders it metaphysically more noncommittal than traditional philosophical theology.

Of course, it can be pointed out that when Kant wrote the time was not yet ripe for these various forms of spiritualized Spinozism, which, indeed, became possible only through the philosophical revolution he himself initiated. From a more strictly philosophical point of view, however, a specifically theistic response to man's moral predicament was suggested to Kant by the inevitable problems of transcendent metaphysics. Kant viewed the concept of God, along with the concepts of free will and the soul's immortality, as necessary ideas for theoretical reason, and the question of God's existence as one of reason's eternally insoluble problems. Man's practical dilemma gives to this problem a new dimension and a new urgency. For a world governed by a wise providence would be a just world, in which our moral endeavors could be expected to bear fruit. The belief in such a providence, a belief suggested but wholly unsubstantiated by the pretended science of rational theology, thus becomes the most natural way of conceiving the possibility of our highest moral end.

From this point of view, then, Kant's justification of theism must be sought not only in the moral and existential considerations leading to practical faith, but also in the theoretical dialectic which is supposed to furnish this faith with a clear and compelling conception of its natural object.

2. J. G. Fichte, *Werke*, ed. F. Medicus (Leipzig, 1910), 3:130.

Like the other ideas of reason, the idea of God arises for Kant from an attempt to think the "unconditioned" in respect to appearances which must always be given as "conditioned" in some specific manner. In the Antinomies, Kant argues that we arrive at the idea of a "necessary being" by tracing a series of contingent or causally dependent beings back to the idea of its unconditional source, in a manner closely analogous to the causal series of events which gives rise to the idea of a spontaneous cause or free will. In Kant's view, however, the concept of a necessary being is not a satisfactory concept of a God. For properly speaking the concept of God must be the concept of a supremely perfect being, and—for the purposes of moral faith—a being of supreme moral perfection. But Kant did not believe that any other attributes of a necessary being could be deduced from its necessity.

Descartes, along with various other scholastics and rationalists, had argued that the concept of a supremely perfect being is presupposed by the concepts of less perfect things. Kant's account of the origin and rational necessity of the idea of God is a version of their argument. As Kant presented it, the argument owes more to Leibniz than to Descartes, but its precise formulation is in fact original with Kant. The rationalist setting of Kant's reasoning on this point, however, has made it far from popular with his readers, and particularly his English-speaking ones. For Norman Kemp Smith, the opening section of the Ideal of Pure Reason contains "quite the most archaic piece of rationalistic argument in the entire *Critique*." Peter Strawson finds it "hard . . . to feel any sympathy with the suggestion that the idea of a supremely real being arises naturally in this way." In his recent study of the Dialectic, Jonathan Bennett dismisses the whole account in less than a paragraph as "an unconvincing tale." [3]

Kant's derivation of the idea of God is "archaic" in the sense that a long tradition of metaphysical thinking stands behind it. But it is not a mere throwback to a "dogmatic" rationalism, or a

3. Norman Kemp Smith, *A Commentary to Kant's Critique of Pure Reason* (London, 1918), p. 522. Peter F. Strawson, *The Bounds of Sense* (London, 1966), p. 222. Jonathan Bennett, *Kant's Dialectic*, p. 282.

piece of reasoning whose spirit and substance are at odds with Kant's critical thought. What Kant's more empiricist readers have often had trouble grasping (or perhaps rather accepting) is that Kant's empiricism in the theory of knowledge was not of a kind which prevented him from retaining a high degree of sympathy with the rationalist problematic. Kant's criticism of rationalist "dogmatism" was anything but a contemptuous rejection of its metaphysical questions, after the Humean or the positivist fashion. On the contrary, it is an attempt to understand these problems and their philosophical sources better than the rationalists themselves had been able to do. No doubt it is difficult for someone with a contemptuous attitude toward the rational theology of the pre-Kantian tradition to find much of interest in Kant's treatment of the same issues. But anyone who thinks it worth the time to study what Aquinas, Scotus, Descartes, Spinoza, or Leibniz thought about the concept of a supremely perfect being should also find something of interest in Kant's critical discussion of this same idea.

The Ideal of Pure Reason

Kant's Ontology

Kant's conception of God and his theory of the rational origin of this conception both depend heavily on ontological views which are part of a tradition which goes back at least to Plato. According to this tradition, reality or being admits of degrees or amounts. Some things have more of it than others, and the more reality a thing has, the better and more perfect a thing it is. Things can be arranged on something like a scale, according to the degree of their being or perfection. God, the *ens realissimum*, has the greatest possible being; he alone is or exists totally and unqualifiedly. Other things participate in being to various degrees and in various ways, and these differences constitute the qualitative distinctions between these things.

Such views can hardly be called popular today. But perhaps they are out of favor less because there are insuperable objections to them than because they fail to accord with our current metaphysical prejudices. Perhaps the most natural worry about the traditional ontology is how it can make sense to speak in comparative terms about being or reality. Hobbes raised this point in his objections to Descartes' use of such language in the *Meditations*. "Does reality admit of more or less?" he asked. "Or if [M. Descartes] thinks that one thing can be more a thing than another, let him consider how it is possible for this to be rendered clear to the mind."[4] Hobbes's puzzlement seems to be based on the idea that whether something exists, or is a thing, is merely a matter of yes or no, and cannot intelligibly be treated as a question of more or less. A thing either exists or it does not. There is no third possibility. To questions like: "Are leprechauns real?" and "Does a flying horse exist?" it makes no sense to answer: "To some degree." Perhaps Hobbes suspected Descartes of falling into this kind of nonsense.

But the traditional ontology need be at no loss for responses to Hobbes here. A strongly Platonistic adherent to it, for instance, will insist that some things, such as the denizens of the world of appearance and becoming, are indeed neither truly real nor wholly unreal, but must be accorded an ontological status somewhere between full being and utter nonbeing. A different reply to such worries was given by St. Thomas Aquinas. In response to the objection that "being cannot receive more and less," he distinguished between "absolute being," which a thing either has or lacks according as it is either an actual substance or not; and "relative being," which a thing has to the extent that it possesses "superadded actuality" in the form of some virtue or perfection.[5] For Aquinas, whether a thing exists absolutely (whether it is a substance) is a yes or no question. But he nevertheless maintained that the differing degrees of perfection or actuality among (real or possible) substances permit us to regard them as having more or less being relative to one another or to some standard. A horse, for instance, is a better horse, and *more* a horse, insofar as it possesses a greater degree of strength, swiftness, courage, and intelligence. And anything, whatever

4. René Descartes, *Oeuvres*, ed. C. Adam and P. Tannery (Paris, 1904), 7:185. Cf. *Philosophical Works*, ed. Haldane and Ross (New York, 1955), 2:71.
5. *Summa Theologiae* Ia Q. 5, a. 1, ad 2, 3.

its nature, is a greater being, and has (relatively) more being insofar as it contains more of actuality or reality. A horse, possessing the actuality of life, has greater relative being than any inanimate thing; a man, possessing the actuality of reason, has a higher degree of being than any beast. And God, whose essence is pure actuality, has the greatest possible relative being. God's being, for Aquinas, is in fact the standard by which the relative being of other things is measured.

In the Ideal of Pure Reason, Kant introduces his own version of the traditional ontology via his account of the content of the predicates employed in judgments: "The judgments our reason makes about things are either affirmative or negative. That is, when I predicate something of a thing, this predicate I apply to the thing expresses either that something is (or is met with) in the thing, or else that something is not in it. A predicate which expresses being in a thing contains a *reality*, but one which expresses nonbeing contains its negation."[6] Kant's point here does not have to do with the logical form of predicates, but with what he calls their "transcendental content," "such content as can be thought a priori as belonging to them." When we consider predicates with respect to such content,

we find that through some of them is represented a being, and through others a mere nonbeing. Logical negation, which is indicated simply through the little word *not*, does not really depend on a concept, but only on the relation of one to another in a judgment. . . . A transcendental negation, on the contrary, signifies nonbeing in itself and is opposed to transcendental affirmation, which is a Something, the very concept of which in itself expresses a being; hence it is called reality (thinghood) because only through it, and as far as it reaches, are objects somethings (things).[7]

Kemp Smith holds that Kant's use of the traditional ontology in the Ideal of Pure Reason is incompatible with the critical doctrines in the Analytic of the first critique. "In order to make this argument at all convincing he is constrained to treat as valid the presupposed ontology, though that has already been shown in

6. *Gesammelte Schriften*, 28, 2, 2, p. 1013; *Lectures on Philosophical Theology*, p. 44.
7. *Critique of Pure Reason*, A 574f/B 602f.

the discussion of the *Amphiboly* to be altogether untenable." "The teaching of the *Analytic*," he concludes, "will no more combine with this scholastic rationalism than oil with water."[8] But Kemp Smith is thoroughly mistaken here. In the Amphiboly discussion to which he refers, there is no criticism of the traditional ontology, but only an attack on Leibniz's identification of real and logical possibility.[9]

The traditional ontology lies behind even so fundamental a part of the Analytic as the three categories of quality: reality, negation, and limitation. A "reality" for Kant is a quality whose transcendental content consists in some determinate kind of being, actuality, or perfection. A "negation" consists in the lack or absence of some determinate reality. And a "limitation" consists in a certain degree of reality or the presence of some reality or realities taken together with the absence of others. The same ontology is endorsed again in the Schematism, where the schema of reality is said to be the "magnitude or quantum of something insofar as it fills time." In the Anticipations of Perception, this ontology is back of the claim that "the real" which is given in experience must always be an "intensive magnitude."[10]

If Kant's endorsement of the traditional ontology is unambiguous, the exact character of this ontology in its Kantian form is not so easy to make out, and some of Kant's ways of expressing himself tend rather to blur the picture than to clarify it. Sometimes he refers to "kinds of reality" and speaks as if "realities" are qualitatively distinct properties, each admitting of different degrees or magnitudes. On this view, "power" might be one reality among others. It would be found pure and whole in God's omnipotence, and to lesser degrees in the limited powers of various creatures. But it would be qualitatively distinct from other realities. At other times, however, Kant speaks of things as "compounds of realities and negations." The idea thus suggests itself that realities are supposed to be "quanta" or "atoms" of being, so to speak; and that a thing has more of a given perfection the more of these atoms it has. God's omnipotence

8. Kemp Smith, *Commentary*, p. 524f.
9. *Critique of Pure Reason*, A 273/B 329. See below, pp. 56–59.
10. *Critique of Pure Reason*, A 143/B 182, A 166/B 207; cf. A 208/B 254.

would thus presumably consist in his having all the realities of a certain sort (all the "powers"); and the more powerful of his creatures would have a larger selection of these realities than the less powerful.[11]

But Kant insists both in the Schematism and in the Anticipations of Perception that "the real which is an object of sensation" admits of a *continuum* of intensive magnitudes. This, together with Kant's reference to realities as magnitudes of "the real" and to "degrees of reality" (in the singular), conjures up the further picture of reality as a kind of homogeneous "stuff," perhaps captured in determinate amounts (different "realities" in the plural) and in that form constituting the transcendental content of predicates. This seems, at first glance anyway, to have been Kant's view in his 1759 essay on optimism. For there he says that different realities are distinguished one from another "not in respect of their constitution (*qualitate*) but in respect of their magnitude (*gradu*)."[12] Yet by this Kant appears to mean only that no two realities can have exactly identical positive contents (a version of Leibniz's principle of the identity of indiscernibles). Thus he insists that "realities are distinguished from one another through nothing but the negations, absences, and limits appended to one of them." But this is not necessarily to deny that realities can be limited in different *ways*. And in his 1763 essay on negative quantities, Kant argues that two realities can differ in such a way as to cancel each other out through a *Realrepugnanz* (as in the case of equal magnitude acting in opposite directions). This seems to suggest that realities can be *equal* in magnitude and yet *differ* in magnitude (as +3 is a magnitude equal to, but different from, -3).[13]

11. *Critique of Pure Reason*, A 577/B 605. The same account is suggested also by Wolff: "A most perfect being is said to be one in which all compossible realities are in the absolutely highest degree" (*Theologia naturalis* [Frankfurt and Leipzig, 1737] 2:4).

12. *Gesammelte Schriften*, 2:31.

13. *Gesammelte Schriften*, 2:172–174. England believes that the 1763 essay represents an "abandonment of the quantitative view of reality" in favor of a "qualitative" one (*Kant's Conception of God* [New York, 1966], p. 68). And it is true that the notion of a "real opposition" between realities is a new development there. But the very title of the essay on negative quantities indicates that Kant still conceived of reality as admitting of degrees or amounts, and its whole

Perhaps the different strands of Kant's ontological theory can be brought together using a picture he himself suggests. In the first critique, Kant says that "all the manifoldness of things is only a multifarious way of limiting the concept of highest reality, which is their common substratum, just as all figures are possible only as different ways of limiting infinite space." [14] In the *Lectures on Philosophical Theology* he employs a slightly different analogy, comparing reality with light and negation with shadow. In one of the manuscript versions of these lectures, these two pictures are combined: "For example, if there were an eternal light, filling all of space, then no point would be in shadow. But now if we think of something bringing about a shadow, then there would arise a thing which is bounded (*appliziert*) with negation." [15]

Let us picture "the real" as an expanse of what we may call "ontological space." Different degrees or magnitudes of reality may be pictured as limited volumes of this space, portions of it which may differ in size, shape, and location. Each of the "kinds" of reality may be thought of as a specific region of this space, occupying a definite location within the ontological space as a whole, and standing in a determinate relation to each of the other regions. In this way, we can account for "qualitative" differences between different realities, without violating the principle that realities should differ only in degree, that is, in the nature of their respective limitations. At the same time, we can represent one reality's exceeding another in degree by picturing the greater reality as a portion of ontological space which properly encloses the portion corresponding to the smaller reality. [16]

---

purpose was to relate this ontological point to the use of negative quantities in physics and other sciences. See below, p. 58.

14. *Critique of Pure Reason*, A 578/B 606.

15. *Gesammelte Schriften*, 28, 2, 2, p. 1005; *Lectures on Philosophical Theology*, p. 34. *Gesammelte Schriften*, 28, 2, 2, pp. 1146f. Cf. Refl. 5270, *Gesammelte Schriften*, 18:139.

16. I choose this way of putting the matter because such comparisons are normally made between qualitatively similar properties, as when it is said that Achilles exceeds Odysseus in strength, but Odysseus exceeds Achilles in cleverness. But can we also compare the amount or magnitude of reality in two properties which are qualitatively distinct? Can we, in other words, try to decide which has more relative being, the cleverness of Odysseus or the strength of

And of course the degrees of reality on this picture will be continuous magnitudes, just as spatial regions are.

Following Kant's picture, then, each possible thing may be represented by a certain "lighted" portion of ontological space, with the remainder of this space left in "shadow" or "darkness." Likewise, the transcendental content of every predicate corresponds to some portion of ontological space, having a positive volume and a specific location. If the predicate is a "reality," then it says of the subject to which it is applied that the corresponding portion of space is "lighted" with respect to that subject. If it is a "negation," then it says that the corresponding portion is "dark" with respect to the subject. Negations, while informative about things, cannot by themselves constitute the concept of a possible thing, because they tell us only which portions of ontological space are "dark" with respect to it, while the thing is constituted by the "lighted" portions. And of course a space which is entirely in darkness corresponds to nothing whatever: "the concept *de ente omni modo negativo* is the concept of a *non entis*." [17]

The Cartesian Argument

In the Third Meditation, Descartes maintains that the idea of God has a special and fundamental place among all his ideas, that "in some way the perception of the infinite is in me prior to that of the finite, that is, the idea of God prior to that of myself." His argument for this claim is based on the traditional ontology, on the fact that "more reality is contained in the infinite substance than in the finite." "For," says Descartes, "from what ground could I understand that I doubt, that I desire, that is,

---

Achilles? Nothing in Kant appears to furnish an answer to this question. The spatial metaphor, however, can be adapted to either a positive or a negative answer. If we decide that such comparisons can be made, then we could represent the amount of reality in different properties as the spatial volume enclosed by the corresponding regions of ontological space. If we decide that only qualitatively similar realities can be compared as to their magnitude, then we can refuse to admit any analogy to the notion of a volume of space, taken as an absolute magnitude, and instead admit comparisons only in cases where the regions share a common location.

17. *Gesammelte Schriften*, 28, 2, 2, p. 1013; *Lectures on Philosophical Theology*, p. 44; cf. *Critique of Pure Reason*, A 575/B 603.

that something is not in me and that I am in general imperfect, if there were in me no idea of a more perfect being, by comparison with which I might come to know my defects?"[18]

Kant also maintains that the idea of God is a fundamental one for human reason, and that its origin in human thought is "as a standard according to which [reason] can make determinations." Kant's defense of this at times seems to be along the same lines as Descartes':

But what are negations? They are nothing but limitations of realities. For no negation can be thought unless the positive has been thought previously. How could I think of a mere deficiency, of darkness without a concept of light, or poverty without a concept of prosperity? Thus if every negative concept is derived in that it always presupposes a reality, then as a consequence every thing in its thorough determination as an *ens partim reale, partim negativum* presupposes an *ens realissimum*.[19]

It would be a mistake to think that either Descartes or Kant mean to say that in our minds the idea of God must literally precede in time the ideas of other things, as if all newborn children have to be rational theologians before they can occupy their thoughts with more mundane matters. The "priority" ascribed to the idea of the infinite is not a temporal one. Rather, the claim is that the idea of God is somehow implicit in or presupposed by our concepts of less perfect things, whether or not this presupposition is explicitly recognized. Kant, in fact, is concerned precisely with the way in which reason *generates* this idea in its attempt to think "the unconditioned" in relation to what is given as conditioned in our experience.

The Cartesian argument is based on the principle that the concepts of negative properties presuppose concepts of positive ones: to have the concept of what is not F, one must also have the concept of F. If I conceive myself as lacking in some power or capacity, I must know what it would be to have that power. If I think of myself as ignorant in some respect or other, I must have some conception of what it would be to have the knowledge that I lack. But, it may be objected, such considerations

18. *Oeuvres*, 7:45–46, cf. *Philosophical Works* 1:166.
19. *Gesammelte Schriften*, 28, 2, 2, pp. 44f; *Lectures on Philosophical Theology*, pp. 1013f.

establish no priority of the concept of power over that of impotence or of knowledge over ignorance: for in fact the concepts of contradictory opposites go together, their presupposition is mutual. If the concept of not-F presupposes the concept of F, it is equally true that I cannot really have the concept of F without having that of not-F.[20]

There is some force in this objection, but its way of disposing of the Cartesian argument is a bit too quick. For once we accept the traditional ontology, we must admit that of every pair of contradictory predicates one ascribes some portion of reality to the subject (or specifies some portion of "ontological space" as "lighted" in respect of it), while the other simply denies this same portion (or specifies the same portion of space as "dark" in respect of it). The content of *both* predicates thus consists in the reality affirmed by one of them and denied by the other. Since the concept of each predicate presupposes that of the other, both presuppose two concepts: the concept of the portion of reality in question, and the concept "not." The status of these two presupposed concepts, however, is very different. The former one serves to identify the specific content of both contradictory predicates; the mere concept "not," presupposed equally by any and every pair of contradictories, does not serve to identify any particular concept whatever. From this point of view, then, the specific content of any pair of contradictory predicates is identified by the portion of reality included in the positive member of that pair. The negative member adds nothing of interest, but only the notion of negation in general, which is presupposed by every concept whatsoever. The Cartesian argument, therefore, seems to be on firm ground when it insists that the concept of any negation, lack, or imperfection must be founded on the concept of the corresponding reality.

Yet this argument is in trouble elsewhere. For merely from the fact that every concept of negation presupposes the concept of the corresponding reality, it does not follow that the concept of every finite thing presupposes the concept of a most real being. It may be that I can only have the concept of something which is not-F if I have the concept of F; but it is not equally evident that I cannot have the concept of something which is partly F, or F to some degree, without the concept of something wholly, unqualifiedly, and maximally F. It may be, for instance, that I cannot have a concept of some ignorance (or the mere lack of some piece of knowledge) unless I have some concept of that piece of knowledge. But it is not equally evident that I cannot have a concept of limited knowledge without having a concept of omniscience. I may recognize that my knowledge is limited simply by realizing that it might grow in certain (finite) respects, or that I may be mistaken in some of the things I presently think I know. There is no need in this case to contrast my limited knowledge with omniscience, as there was the need for me to contrast my not knowing some definite thing with the possibility of knowing it. This is why, prima facie at least, my concept of my limited knowledge is not threatened even if I suppose that it might increase endlessly, without ever attaining to any maximum, and even if there should be no such possibility as "omniscience" for it to aim at. Thus far from demonstrating that the concept of a most real being is presupposed by the concept of every finite thing, the Cartesian argument even falls short of providing us with any motive for thinking that such a concept can be coherently formed. If this is the sort of argument by which Kant means to account for our concept of God, then we cannot be too hopeful about its prospects of success.

Complete Individual Concepts

In fact, however, Kant does not rely merely on the Cartesian argument. His line of thinking is both more complex and more Leibnizian in character. For Kant, the idea of an *ens realissimum* has its origin in the attempt of reason to form a conception of the most fundamental condition of the possibility of particular things, a condition which he calls their "thorough determination." In Kant's terminology, a "determination" is any property or quality, the content of some predicate. The verb "to determine" is used in two related senses, one of them epistemological, the other ontological. To "determine" a thing with respect to a given predicate is to decide by some rational procedure whether or not that predicate applies to it, or belongs to its concept. On the other hand, in the ontological sense, the concept of a thing is said to be "determined" with respect to a pair of contradictory predicates if one of these predicates belongs to that concept and the other is excluded from it. Some concepts are thoroughly determined, that is, determined with respect to every possible pair of contradictory predicates. Other concepts are determined only partially, and left indeterminate with respect to some predicates. Completely determined concepts are concepts of individual things; concepts which are only partially determined are concepts of universals.

Kant's immediate source for these views is Wolff and Baumgarten. According to the latter, "the complex of all determinations compossible in a being is its THOROUGH DETERMINATION. Hence a being is either determined thoroughly, or determined less than this. The former is a particular (an individual), the latter a universal."[21] Kant illustrates this distinction in the *Lectures on Philosophical Theology*. The concept of a human being, he says, "does not determine whether this human being is young or old, tall or short, learned or unlearned."[22] Hence the concept "human being" is not determined with respect to these pairs of predicates, and is consequently the concept of a universal. But a particular human being, for example, Socrates, must be either young or old, tall or short, learned or unlearned. The concept of Socrates as a concrete individual must be determined with respect to every possible pair of contradictory predicates. In the same vein, Wolff insists that "whatever exists or is actual is thoroughly determined." Further, he maintains that the "thorough determination inhering in actual beings is their principle of individuation or thisness (*haecceitas*)."[23]

Obviously the real author of all these ideas is Leibniz, with his conception of the "complete notion" of every individual, containing everything that ever was, is, or will be true of that individual: "For in the perfect notion of each individual substance

21. *Metaphysica* (Halle, 1963) §148.
22. *Gesammelte Schriften*, 28, 2, 2, p. 1014; *Lectures on Philosophical Theology*, p. 44.
23. Wolff, *Gesammelte Werke* (Halle, 1962) 2, 3, pp. 187–89. Cf. Baumgarten, *Metaphysica*, §§53, 151.

there are contained all its predicates, both necessary and contingent, past, present, and future." It is from Leibniz too that Wolff, Baumgarten, and Kant derive the idea that the *omnimoda determinatio* of a concept is what makes it the concept of a particular thing rather than of a universal, and constitutes the principle of individuation for that thing:

> It is the nature of an individual substance, or complete being, to have a notion so complete that it is sufficient to contain, and render deducible from itself, all the predicates of the subject to which this notion is attributed. On the other hand, an accident is a being whose notion does not include all that can be attributed to the subject to which this notion is attributed. Take, for example, the quality of being a king, which belongs to Alexander the Great. This quality, when abstracted from its subject, is not sufficiently determinate for an individual and does not contain the other qualities of the same subject, nor everything that the notion of this prince contains. God, on the other hand, seeing the individual notion or *haecceitas* of Alexander, sees in it at the same time the foundation of and reason for all the predicates which can truly be stated of him.[24]

But perhaps it will be thought that Kant has no business endorsing these extravagant metaphysical ideas. For did he not reject, with good reason, the Leibnizian view that all truths are analytic? Did he not insist that all our genuine knowledge, the a priori part as well as the empirical, concerns synthetic propositions, whose predicate is not contained in the concept of its subject and cannot by any means be analyzed out of it?

It is true that Kant denied that any of our knowledge results from the analysis of concepts. As early as the *Nova dilucidatio* essay of 1755 Kant began to take issue with the received Leibnizian views on this. In treating of the rationalist principle of sufficient reason, Kant distinguished *rationes cur*, the reasons or causes which explain *why* a determination inheres in a subject, from *rationes quod*, reasons for thinking *that* something is so, or grounds for our knowledge that the subject is determined in

---

24. Leibniz, *Philosophische Schriften*, ed. C. J. Gerhardt (Berlin, 1890), 7:311, 4:433ff. *Philosophical Writings*, ed. Parkinson (London, 1973), pp. 77, 17ff. Kant, however, appears not to count relational properties (e.g. being a king) as determinations essential to the individuation of a thing, since his theory makes no provision for them.

such a way. *Rationes cur* are also called *rationes antecedenter deter-minans*, while *rationes quod* are said to be *consequenter determinans*. The former sort of reason determines a subject "antecedently" (ontologically) in the constitution of the subject itself; but it does not provide *us* with any way of determining the subject or knowing its properties. Our knowledge instead must proceed "consequently" from some concept and advance by *rationes quod* to determine this concept further.[25]

In his critical writings, Kant insisted that the principle of contradiction, "the supreme principle of all analytic judgments," provides us only with a *conditio sine qua non* of truth, and is not (as the Leibnizians had claimed) a principle from which genuine a priori knowledge can be derived.[26] Analytic judgments, according to Kant, are those in which the predicate is "contained in" the concept of the subject. In synthetic judgments, on the other hand, the predicate cannot be found among these contents. Analytic judgments serve only to explicate or clarify our concepts, and do not (in themselves) give us any knowledge. For even the concepts on whose contents these judgments depend presuppose a priori synthesis through which alone knowledge first arises.[27]

But Kant's divergence from the Leibnizian tradition on this point, although important, tends to obscure his agreement with it on related ones. For Kant all our knowledge proceeds from various concepts with a given content to a further "determination" of these concepts, through the "addition" to them of predicates not to be found already in their content. (In the case of empirical knowledge, the addition is grounded on the experience of an object to which the concept refers; in the case of synthetic a priori knowledge, it is based on the conditions of possible experience.) Yet, says Kant, although the predicate in a synthetic judgment is not "contained in" the concept of the subject, if the judgment is true this predicate is "connected with" that concept and thus "belongs to" it. "For even though I do not

25. *Gesammelte Schriften*, 1:388–390. Cf. England, *Kant's Conception of God*, pp. 220–222.
26. *Critique of Pure Reason*, A 59/B 84, A 150/B 189.
27. *Critique of Pure Reason*, A 9f/B 13f.

include the predicate . . . in the concept [of the subject], yet this concept still signifies the complete experience [of the object] through one of its parts; and thus I can add other parts of this experience to this first part, as something belonging to it." "Although the one concept is not contained in the other, nevertheless they belong to one another, if only contingently, as parts of one whole."[28] All our concepts, according to Kant, are "partial concepts" because they are not completely determined individual representations, but only discursive representations which "signify" the whole experience of a fully determinate individual without encompassing its complete determination in their content. As we add new predicates (synthetically) to some universal concept through which we signify a given individual, we advance toward the complete determination of that individual.

Thus, while repudiating the view that all truths are analytic, Kant retains several important ideas which are involved in the Leibnizian theory of complete individual concepts. First, he pictures the real constitution of every individual as a complete whole made up of all the predicates which will ever be true of that individual. Second, he regards this whole as involving the thorough determination of the individual, that is, its (ontological) determination with respect to every possible pair of contradictory predicates. And finally, he retains the Leibnizian ideal of knowledge as the thorough (epistemological) determination of the individual known. On this point especially there is no real disagreement between Kant and the Leibnizians. For of course neither Leibniz nor any of his followers ever believed that our knowledge of contingent truths of fact about individuals is founded on the analysis of their individual concepts. For the Leibnizians, as for Kant, the complete determination of an individual is an infinite task, one which we can never in principle complete. The only difference is that for Leibniz this is an infinite task of analysis (analogous to the decimal expansion of an irrational number); whereas for Kant it is a task of synthesis, an assimilation and systematization of information based on intuitions, concepts, and the judgments and inferences made possible by them.

28. *Critique of Pure Reason*, A 8, B 12.

The Principle of Thorough Determination

Leibniz describes the entire collection of complete notions of individuals, as it is found in God's understanding, as the "country of possibles."[29] He apparently thinks that the very possibility of an individual somehow depends on or consists in the fact that the divine intellect represents this notion of this individual as complete or thoroughly determined. And Kant seems to be following up this hint when he formulates the "principle of thorough determination," which he treats as a transcendental principle underlying the real possibility of individual things. "Every thing," Kant tells us, "as regards its possibility, stands under the principle of *thorough* determination, according to which, of all the *possible* predicates of *things*, in comparison with their opposites, one of them must belong to it."

Kant is at pains to distinguish this principle from the principle of excluded middle. But his attempt to do so is not easy to make out. He describes the principle of excluded middle as a "principle of *determinability*," governing every *concept* "with regard to what is not contained in it." According to it, "only one of every two contradictorily opposed predicates can belong to a concept. This principle is based on the law of contradiction and is therefore a merely logical principle."[30] Yet the principle that *at most* one of any two contradictories can belong to a given concept is not merely "based on" the principle of contradiction, it simply *is* that principle. The principle of excluded middle is rather the complementary principle which says that *at least* one of any pair of contradictories must belong to any given subject. No one, however, would think of applying this principle to universal concepts with respect to pairs of contradictories which lie outside their content. For this would be to argue, as a matter of logic, that the concept of humanity in general is determined with respect to the opposites "young/not young," "wise/not wise," and so on. The principle of excluded middle, therefore, seems to be intelligible only if we suppose it to apply to individual things, whose concepts must always be determined with

29. *Philosophische Schriften*, 2:42; cf. *Philosophical Writings*, p. 56.
30. *Critique of Pure Reason*, A 571/B 599.

respect to every pair of contradictories. Interpreted in this way, however, the merely logical principle of excluded middle seems to be exactly the same as Kant's supposedly transcendental principle of thorough determination.

The crucial point to be kept in mind, however, is that the logical principles of contradiction and excluded middle only give us instructions concerning the possibility of determining a concept with respect to any given pair of contradictories. The former principle says that a concept can be determined by at most one member of any such pair, and the latter says that for any individual concept, one member of any given pair of contradictories must belong to it. Neither principle says anything about the sum-total of such pairs considered as a whole, or even requires us to suppose that such talk makes sense. The principle of thorough determination, however, holds that the real possibility of an individual thing depends on the completeness of its individual concept, on the possibility of bringing together in one notion the unique combination of predicates which identify it as the particular thing it is. This principle, therefore, unlike the principle of excluded middle, does require us to consider all pairs of contradictory predicates, taken as a whole. In Kant's words, the principle of thorough determination, "everything existing is thoroughly determined," "does not mean that one of every pair of *given* contradictories must belong to it, but that one of every pair of all *possible* predicates must belong to it   The *determinability* of every *concept* is subordinate to the *universality* (*universalitas*) of the principle of excluded middle between two contradictory predicates; but the *determination* of a *thing* is subordinated to the *allness* (*universitas*) of the sum of all possible predicates."[31] In Kant's view, moreover, to conceive the possibility of an individual thing is to imagine what it might be like actually to determine it thoroughly (that is, to imagine some rational procedure by which it might be known which of every possible pair of contradictories belongs to it). Neither the principle of contradiction nor the principle of excluded middle, however, tells us anything about what such a procedure might be like, nor do they in any way require us to worry about such

31. *Critique of Pure Reason*, A 572/B 600.

frightening questions. The principle of thorough determination, however, by insisting that the real possibility of an individual thing depends on the possibility of its complete notion, does force us to worry about them.

Absolute Real Possibility

But perhaps just at the moment some other questions worry us more: What does Kant mean by the claim that the possibility of an individual thing depends on its relation to the *universitas* of all possible predicates? What sort of possibility is he talking about? And why does he think his principle of thorough determination is true?

According to Kant, modal concepts (that is, possibility, actuality, necessity) never express any real properties of the things of which they are predicated, but express instead a relation of those things to a mind or mental faculty which considers them. (This belief is behind his rejection of the ontological argument and is also what he means when he says that the a priori principles of modality are not "objectively synthetic.")[32] Kant normally distinguishes between *logical* possibility, which consists in the absence of contradiction from a concept, and *real* possibility, which requires something over and above this.

For Kant, all possibility consists in "thinkability," in some sense or other of that term. But of course this never means that possibility depends on merely psychological considerations. Thinkability, in the sense relevant to possibility, has to do with the relation of the concept through which something is thought to the necessary rules and conditions governing the operations of the faculty which thinks it. This is clear in the case of logical possibility, which for Kant consists in the noncontradictoriness of a concept. A contradictory concept is not thinkable in the sense that to form such a concept is already to violate one of the basic principles of general logic, or "absolutely necessary rules of thought without which there can be no employment of the understanding whatever."[33] To think is to employ the understanding. To attempt to think a contradictory concept is to vio-

32. *Critique of Pure Reason*, A 219/B 266.
33. *Critique of Pure Reason*, A 52/B 76.

late an absolutely necessary rule of the understanding, and hence not really to employ it at all. Hence to think a contradictory concept is not really to think, and every such concept is in that sense "unthinkable."

In the Postulates of Empirical Thought, Kant describes the real possibility of empirical objects as the agreement of their concept with the formal conditions of possible experience, as laid down by the truths of mathematics and the synthetic laws of pure understanding (such as the principle of causality). Here possibility means the thinkability of an object as a candidate for possible empirical knowledge.[34] As the title of this part of the *Critique* suggests, the possibility in question is empirical thinkability. Kant does not of course mean that transcendent objects (those, such as a free cause, whose concepts do not agree with the formal conditions of possible experience) are all (really) impossible. Rather he means only that such objects are not possible as objects of our empirical knowledge. And since for Kant all our knowledge of objects depends on the conditions of their experienceability by us, it follows that the real possibility or impossibility of transcendent objects is something unknowable by us.

It is noteworthy, however, that in the Postulates, Kant puts even narrower restrictions on our empirical employment of the concept of real possibility. Our use of this concept, he says, must always be relative to what has been given in actual perception. The realm of *knowable* empirical possibility, in his view, never includes what merely would have occurred had some contrary-to-fact condition been satisfied, even if that condition itself in no wise contradicts the formal criteria of possible experience. Suppose, for instance, that Caesar would still have been emperor on the calends of April if Brutus had not stabbed him on the ides of March. Now it would in no way have violated the formal conditions of possible experience if Brutus had not stabbed Caesar on the ides of March, and hence we may be tempted to conclude that Caesar might very well have been emperor on the calends of April, and that it now remains a real

34. H. J. Paton argues that, contrary to first appearances, there is nothing viciously circular about this exposition of empirical possibility. *Kant's Metaphysic of Experience* (London, 1936) 2:354ff.

possibility that he still should have been emperor then. But according to Kant, "what is possible only under conditions which are themselves merely possible is not in all respects possible," or "absolutely possible."[35] Rather it is called "possible" only relative to these (contrary to fact) conditions. But then the same is true of the contrary-to-fact condition itself: Brutus would only have failed to stab Caesar if some further contrary-to-fact condition had been satisfied (e.g., if Brutus had changed his mind, or if Caesar had been persuaded by Calpurnia's dream not to go to the Senate on the ides of March). If one is speaking of empirically knowable real possibilities, therefore, every possibility is only possible relative to certain (factual or contrary-to-fact) suppositions. Nothing, according to Kant, can be known to be possible "absolutely" and "in all respects."[36]

Kant's target here is all those philosophers who think they can settle the question whether the field of possibility is wider than the field of actuality, and thus whether the actual course of things is necessary or only contingent. In particular, his target is the Leibnizian claim that we can know there are possible worlds different from the actual one. For Kant, this claim is something we can never expect to establish or to refute. From what is given in experience, we can never infer that "more than a single all-inclusive experience is possible; still less can this be

35. *Critique of Pure Reason*, A 232/B 284.

36. In the Dialectic, Kant distinguishes between two diametrically opposed senses of "absolute" as applied to notions like possibility and necessity. In one sense, the "absolutely possible" is that which is possible "in itself" or "internally," considered in abstraction from external circumstances (which may render it impossible). In another sense, the "absolutely possible" is that which is possible "in all respects" or "in every relation" that which no external circumstance could rule out (*Critique of Pure Reason*, A 324f/B 380f). It seems plain that it is the first sense of "absolute" possibility that Kant has in mind in the Postulates. But Kant needlessly confuses the reader by using the phrase "in all respects" in diametrically opposed ways in the two passages. The explanation is that in the passage from the Dialectic Kant is more interested in the concept of absolute necessity than absolute possibility. His aim is to distinguish the concept of that whose existence is "internally" necessary from that whose existence is necessary, considered in its relation to every possibility. As we shall see below, ever since the *Beweisgrund* essay of 1763, Kant had held that the first concept of absolutely necessary existence is wholly illegitimate, while in that essay he argues that God's existence is absolutely necessary, considered in relation to all possible things.

inferred apart from what is given." All such claims about possible worlds, Kant insists, make use of the notion of "absolute possibility," of something which is supposed to be (really) possible "in all respects" and not merely relative to a given course of experience or to certain counterfactual suppositions. "In fact absolute possibility (that which is in all respects valid) is no mere concept of the understanding, and can in no wise be of empirical use; it rather belongs to reason alone, which transcends all possible empirical use of the understanding." The Postulates of Empirical Thought is therefore not the proper place for a discussion of this concept. "Hence we must content ourselves at this point with a merely critical remark, and otherwise leave the matter in some obscurity until the time comes for treating it further."[37]

This last allusion is itself rather obscure, but it *may* refer to the discussion of the principle of thorough determination in the Ideal of Pure Reason. This is in any case the principal place in the Dialectic where the idea of possibility is treated. And the possibility of things which is supposed to be subject to the principle of thorough determination does correspond very closely to the notion of "absolute" possibility which is discussed in the Postulates. It is, as we have seen, not merely a logical possibility, since its principle is not derived from the principles of general logic. It is, therefore, a kind of real possibility. But it is also a concept which "belongs to reason alone" because it is a possibility which applies to things in general, independently of their relation to possible experience. The a priori possibility of an individual thing in general, moreover, seems to fit exactly the Leibnizian conception of possibility, that possibility which is supposed to belong to all the individual inhabitants of every possible world irrespective of the actuality or nonactuality of that world.

If this conjecture is correct, then Kant means the principle of thorough determination to specify the conditions under which an individual thing possesses absolute real possibility. Here as elsewhere, however, possibility for Kant means thinkability and expresses a relation between a thing and the mental faculty

37. *Critique of Pure Reason*, A 231f/B 284f.

which considers it. Absolute possibility, as we have seen, is a concept of reason, and therefore expresses the thinkability of a thing by mere reason, apart from any conditions of the empirical use of the understanding.

To *think* an object is always to form a *concept* of it. Every concept, however, must possess two features: a "form," supplied a priori by some category of the understanding; and a "content" (a connotation or intension), supplied through intuition, in which consists "the possibility of giving it an object to which it has reference."[38] Strictly speaking, however, this account applies only to empirical concepts and to the schematized categories, that is, to concepts through which *knowledge* of objects is possible. For Kant holds that through the pure categories we can *think* objects which can never be *known* by us because no sensible intuition of them can ever be given. Following Kant's own language, we may call such concepts "empty" or "problematic" concepts: they are "empty" because they possess no determinate intuitive content; and they are "problematic" because none of the judgments in which they are predicated of objects can ever be verified or falsified. Our concepts of objects as noumena or things-in-themselves are all concepts of this sort. So are the ideas of reason which generate the problems of the Dialectic.

It is evident that for Kant the concept of absolute real possibility is an empty concept, since no example of an absolutely possible thing can be given (as such) in any intuition. It is equally true, however, that all our concepts of individual things, insofar as we think of such things as absolutely possible, must also be empty concepts. This is clear not only on account of the emptiness of the concept of absolute possibility, but also on account of the kind of thinkability in which the absolute possibility of a thing consists. Absolute possibility consists in the thinkability of a thing by mere reason, apart from any possible empirical use of the understanding. But this means that the concept of a thing as absolutely possible must be a concept of it

38. *Critique of Pure Reason*, A 239/B 298.

which relates to no possible intuition: in other words, an empty concept.

Kant often asserts that many of our empty concepts (the concepts of things as noumena, the ideas of God, freedom and the soul) are *logically* possible (that is, noncontradictory). And it might seem that this is the only sort of possibility which makes sense in the case of empty concepts. For the characteristic of such concepts is that they possess no intuitive content, but consist wholly in an empty form of thought. Consequently, it might seem that the only sort of thinkability which can apply to them is purely formal or logical thinkability, or noncontradictoriness. Yet Kant insists that absolute possibility—the possibility of individual things which is in question in the Ideal of Pure Reason —is a species not of logical but of *real* possibility. Is there any room in Kant's scheme for such a concept of a priori real possibility? Is Kant not simply violating his own principles here?

Once we see how Kant's conception of absolute real possibility may be rescued from these objections, we will be well on the way to seeing why he regards the principle of thorough determination as laying down the conditions for this sort of possibility. It is true that the concept of an individual thing in general, regarded as something thinkable completely a priori, is an empty concept, a concept without any determinate intuitive content. Yet there still is room in this concept for something referring (if only emptily and indeterminately) to such a content. For every such content must be thought by us under the category of reality; and this category must be employed as part of the a priori concept of an individual thing in general, referring as it were to the empty place where the intuitive content of the concept would be found if this concept were a full-blooded empirical one. By itself, however, this fact does not give rise to any new sort of thinkability beyond noncontradictoriness, or any sort of possibility beyond the merely logical.

But we must also keep in mind that this concept is not supposed to be just any concept at all, but is supposed to be an *individual* concept, the concept of a particular thing differentiated from all others. Of course what differentiates an individual from all others must be its unique combination of qualities, its particular realities and negations. And from the empty category of reality alone, we cannot proceed a single step toward any such differentiation. We can, however, include in our concept of an individual thing the requirement that its realities (whatever they may be) must be such as to make it the concept of an individual, and serve to differentiate it as an individual from all other individuals. This requirement, however, goes beyond the mere requirement of noncontradictoriness, which applies to all concepts whatever and corresponds to mere logical possibility. It requires in addition that the realities thought in the concept should be thought of as constituted in such a way as to make it the concept of an individual thing distinct from every other individual thing.

What is it to think a priori of the real content of a concept as constituted in this way? Obviously, the answer is that it is to think of this content as completely determining the concept with respect all possible pairs of contradictory predicates. For, as Leibniz, Wolff, and Baumgarten all have made clear, to think of a concept as undetermined in any respect is to think a universal concept, a concept which can in principle apply to more than one individual thing, and which consequently does not serve to identify an individual thing. To think of an individual thing a priori is therefore necessarily to think of what has a complete concept or is thoroughly determined. The absolute possibility of an individual thing, however, consists in its a priori thinkability. It follows that the principle of absolute real possibility for individual things is their thorough determination with respect to all possible pairs of contradictories.

The *omnitudo realitatis*

To conceive of a thing in general as really possible a priori is to conceive of it as completely determined. In order to give some kind of concreteness to such a conception, Kant tries to imagine what it would be like to be able completely to determine an individual thing a priori; that is, by some rational procedure to specify for all pairs of contradictory predicates which member of each pair belongs to the thing in question. Of course there is no question here of coming up with a real proposal for inquiry. The complete determination of an actual thing (not to mention its complete determination a priori) is something which far transcends our faculty of knowledge. But Kant believes that it is possible to view the principle of thorough determination as an idea of complete knowledge of a particular thing. According to Kant, the principle of thorough determination "means this: that in order to know a thing completely, one must know every possibility, and must determine it thereby, affirmatively or negatively."[39]

The device Kant employs to represent the procedure for obtaining this complete knowledge a priori is the disjunctive syllogism, or inference *modus tollens*: "The logical determination of a concept by reason [he says] rests on a disjunctive syllogism, in which the major premise contains a logical division (the separation of the spheres of a universal concept), the minor premise limits this sphere to one part, and the conclusion determines the concept through it."[40] Kant seems to have in mind a syllogism such as this:

> *Major premise*: Every warm-blooded creature is either bird or mammal.
> *Minor premise*: This warm-blooded creature is not a bird.
> *Conclusion*: Therefore, it is a mammal.

The major premise of this syllogism takes a universal concept ("warm-blooded creature") and divides its "sphere" (or extension) into two mutually exclusive and jointly exhaustive spheres or parts ("bird" and "mammal"). The minor premise limits a particular subject ("this warm-blooded creature," e.g., this duck-billed platypus) to one of these spheres by denying the other (the sphere "bird") of it. The syllogism's conclusion then predicates the remaining sphere of the subject, thus determining it thereby (as "mammal").

According to Kant, the "universal concept" used in the thorough determination of an individual thing is the "universal concept of reality in general." Yet, says Kant, this universal con-

39. *Critique of Pure Reason*, A 573/B 601.
40. *Critique of Pure Reason*, A 576f/B 604f.

cept "cannot be divided a priori, because apart from experience we are acquainted with none of the determinate species of reality which are contained under this genus." It is here, however, that the traditional ontology comes to our rescue. For this ontology tells us that the concept of reality is the concept of an intensive magnitude. Of course, experiences can never present us with anything resembling an infinite or absolutely maximum degree of reality in general. But if, in our attempt to conceive the thorough determination of objects a priori by pure reason, we permit ourselves to conceive of reality as having such a maximum, then we will be able to see the way clear to a solution of our problem. For if we form the conception of a "sum" (*Inbegriff*) comprehending all possible reality within it, then we can represent a priori the division of the universal concept of reality into different species by representing the division of this "sum" into two mutually exclusive parts.

Thus the transcendental major premise for the thorough determination of all things is nothing but the representation of the sum of all reality. It is not merely a concept which comprehends all predicates *under* itself with regard to their transcendental content, but one which comprehends all of them *within* itself. And the thorough determination of every thing rests on the limitation of this All of reality, in that one part of it is ascribed to that thing and the rest is excluded. This agrees with the *either/or* of the disjunctive major premise and the determination of the object through one part of this division in the minor premise.[41]

The Kantian metaphor of "ontological space" is very much alive in this passage. The "sum" or "All" of reality is said to include all realities (the transcendental content of all predicates) *within* itself, just as in the Aesthetic Kant says the one infinite space includes all finite spaces within itself. And the syllogism described in it can perhaps best be presented in terms of the spatial metaphor. Let us imagine ontological space to be partitioned into a "lighted" portion and a "dark" one, as we did earlier. To the lighted portion of space will correspond one set or collection of realities, to which we may give the name F. The complementary portion of space will contain all the rest of the

41. *Critique of Pure Reason*, A 576f/B 604f.

realities, to which we may give the collective name G. Now to any such division of space, there will be exactly one absolutely possible individual A such that both premises of the following syllogism are true:

A is either F or G.
A is not G.
Therefore, A is F.

Now by "A is F" we mean that all the realities in F may be truly predicated of A, and by "A is not G" we mean that none of the realities in G may be predicated of A. Hence by "A is either F or G" we mean that either all the realities in F or all the realities in G may be predicated of A (the "or" may be taken either as exclusive or inclusive; the minor premise of the syllogism obviates the difference). But F and G have been constructed by an exhaustive division of the "sum" of all reality (the whole of ontological space). Hence the syllogism permits us to determine the concept of A thoroughly, with respect to every possible predicate. For given any predicate P, its transcendental content must be drawn in some manner (positively or negatively, conjunctively or disjunctively) from realities contained in F or in G. If for instance P consists in an affirmative disjunction of predicates drawn from F and predicates drawn from G, then we know that P does belong to the concept of A. If it consists in a negative disjunction of the same predicates, then we know it does not. The case is the same for any other predicate, whatever its structure and however complex it may be. By representing the thorough determination of A, the syllogism represents its absolute possibility, or thinkability a priori through a complete concept. For any absolutely possible individual, moreover, there will be exactly one partitioning of ontological space into complementary parts which will permit its complete determination to be represented in the same manner.

Kant was induced to present the complete determination of an individual concept in terms of a disjunctive syllogism largely by his desire to identify each of the three species of dialectic with one of the three forms of syllogistic reasoning recognized by traditional logic. But it is difficult to regard the syllogistic procedure here as anything but a rather clumsy and artificial scholastic device. The whole work of the syllogism is done by its major premise, which employs the concept of a "sum of all reality" and its division into two complementary "spheres" which exactly correspond to the complete concept of the thing to be thoroughly determined. As a matter of fact, this is also the only feature of the syllogism in which Kant is at all interested. In order to form the concept of a thing in its absolute possibility, we must think of it a priori as thoroughly determined with respect to all possible predicates. But our only concept a priori of the content of such predicates is the pure category of reality, as something in general which admits of degrees or magnitudes. And our only chance of forming a concept which is completely determined depends on the supposition that reality in general admits of a supreme degree or highest magnitude, constituting a single whole which can be divided up in such a way that lesser magnitudes can be represented, and completely represented, as incomplete parts of it. The central point, then, is that the idea of an individual thing in its absolute possibility is an idea of reason, in the forming of which "reason employs a transcendental substratum which contains, as it were, the whole store of material from which all possible predicates of things may be taken." The idea of this substratum, as we have seen, is derived from the pure category of reality, by supposing the varying degrees or magnitudes of which reality admits a priori to be merely so many limitations of a supreme degree or highest magnitude of reality. Hence the idea of this substratum "is nothing but the idea of an All of reality (*omnitudo realitatis*). All true negations are then nothing but *limitations*—something they could not be called, were they not founded upon the unlimited (the All)."[42]

Earlier we examined Descartes' argument that the notion of something finite necessarily leads us to the notion of something infinite or supremely perfect because the latter notion is presupposed by the former, which is founded upon it. We rejected this argument on the ground that the concept of something finite does not presuppose the concept of something infinite in

42. *Critique of Pure Reason*, A 575f/B 603f.

the same way that the concept of the absence of some property presupposes the concept of that property itself. Limited knowledge, for instance, may be conceived as knowledge that might grow in certain respects, as well as knowledge which falls short of omniscience. The concept of limited knowledge, in fact, can be perfectly clear and intelligible even if the concept of omniscience is not. But these same grounds will not justify us in rejecting the Kantian argument that the complete determination of an individual presupposes the concept of a "sum of all reality." We might try to evade Kant's argument by saying that the concept of an individual would be thoroughly determined if we said that predicates $F, G, H, \ldots N$ belong to it, and no others do. But in this case it may always be asked how we can be certain that our list of $F, G, H, \ldots N$ determines the individual *completely*. Perhaps there is some pair of contradictory predicates such that neither is included on our list, nor can either be deduced from what the list contains. Kant's point is that only by supposing that our list uniquely specifies some limited degree of reality (some distinct region or portion of "ontological space") can we be sure that it thoroughly determines the individual in question. But the assumption that this has been done presupposes the notion of the "sum of all reality" as a single complete whole. The superiority of the Kantian argument to the Cartesian one lies in the fact that a thing may be limited or finite in any number of ways, so that it may be conceived as "finite" by reference to *any* of them; but it can only be conceived as thoroughly determined in *one* way. Its complete notion must include *all* the ways it is limited, as well as *all* the ways in which it is not. Hence the idea of any individual as thoroughly determined rests on the idea of an *omnitudo realitatis*, a "sum of all reality," through which its thorough determination can be thought.

The *ens realissimum*

The idea of a "sum of all reality," or the image of "ontological space" as a whole to be divided in a different way between light and shadow to represent the constitution of each thing, quite naturally suggests the idea of a thing whose constitution fills the whole of this space, or, in Kant's words, of "an eternal light filling all of space with no point in shadow." And Kant calls the concept of such a being the "ideal of pure reason." An "idea" in Kantian terminology is any concept (such as that of a simple substance or an uncaused cause) which is generated a priori by reason, to which nothing given in experience can correspond. An "ideal," however, is "an idea *in individuo*, i.e., an individual determinable or rather determined through its idea alone."[43] As we have seen above, the thorough determination of any individual thing rests on and presupposes the idea of a sum of all reality, from which the transcendental content of all possible predicates may be derived. For this reason, the complete notion of any individual is said to be "determined through" this idea. In the case of any finite being, however, this idea is necessarily different in content from the notion to be determined. For the idea contains all realities, whereas only some of them belong to any finite individual.

Only an *ens realissimum*, or a being thought of as possessing the sum of all reality, is determined through its *own* concept or idea. Hence the idea of a supreme being or God is "the only genuine ideal of which reason is capable. For only in this case is a concept of a thing, a concept universal in itself, recognized as thoroughly determined through itself." This is what Kant means in the *Lectures on Philosophical Theology* when he says that God is "the only complete thing," because "in this case alone do I have a thing whose thorough determination is bound up with its concept."[44]

Some of Kant's commentators, however, have questioned the legitimacy of this transition from a "sum of all reality" to an *ens realissimum*. According to England, it does follow from Kant's premises "that in the determination of any concept there is presupposed a rational context—a systematic whole in which the particular concept finds its place." But England finds it "bewildering" that Kant insists on thinking of his transcendental ideal as "an *ens realissimum* in the rationalistic sense of the

43. *Critique of Pure Reason*, A 568/B 596.
44. *Critique of Pure Reason*, A 576/B; *Gesammelte Schriften*, 28, 2, 2, p. 1014; cf. *Lectures on Philosophical Theology*, p. 44.

term."[45] England's point here is not merely that the concept of a "sum of all reality" is not the same as the concept of a "most real being," an individual thing possessing this sum. Kant would doubtless admit this much, and content himself with the observation that the idea of a "sum of all reality," particularly taken in its close relation to the thorough determination of individual things, very naturally *suggests* the transcendental ideal of an individual thing which possesses all reality, and is thus thoroughly determined solely through its own concept. England's objection rather is that Kant's ontology does not permit him to move from the concept of a rational "system" or "context" to that of a supremely real thing. Like Kemp Smith, England thinks that the concept of an *ens realissimum* is positively ruled out by Kant's critical views. Both England and Kemp Smith point to the fact that in the Amphiboly Kant says that there might be a *Realrepugnanz* between realities, that realities might "negate" or "limit" one another "really" or causally, as two equal and opposed forces acting on the same body at the same time cancel each other out, and leave the body at rest.[46] In fact, if there is any such real opposition between any two realities, it seems to follow that no being can possess all realities at once. The concept of a "sum of all reality" is therefore not only different from that of an *ens realissimum*, but perhaps properly understood it even precludes the idea of one.

Leibniz offered a proof that "all perfections are compatible with each other, or can be combined in the same subject."[47] In effect, his argument was that two predicates can be incompatible only if one of them affirms something of the subject which the other denies. In terms of the traditional ontology and the metaphor of ontological space, this means that one predicate affirms the subject to be present in a certain location of ontological space (or this location to be "lighted" with respect to the subject), while the other predicate denies that it is present at that same lo-

45. *Kant's Conception of God*, pp. 120f; cf. Kemp Smith, *Commentary*, pp. 524f.
46. *Critique of Pure Reason*, A 273/B 329.
47. *Philosophische Schriften*, 7:261. Cf. *Philosophical Papers and Letters*, ed. L. Loemker (Dordrecht, 1969), p. 167.

cation (or declares that location to be "dark" with respect to the subject). But this situation, according to Leibniz, can never arise regarding any two predicates that express only reality. For any two such predicates will relate to different locations of ontological space, and neither will deny to the subject any portion of that space. Yet if no two realities can be incompatible, then it follows that all realities can coexist compatibly in the same subject.

Kant concedes in both the *Lectures on Philosophical Theology* and the first critique that Leibniz's proof shows that all realities are *logically* compatible in the same subject, that is, that no contradiction results from the supposition that the same subject possesses all of them. But in Kant's view Leibniz fails to show that an *ens realissimum* is really possible, because his proof does not establish the real or causal compatibility of all realities. If the causal properties of realities are such as to preclude or "cancel" each other, then it will be impossible for all of them to subsist in the same subject, and an *ens realissimum* will be impossible despite the fact that there is no contradiction in its concept.

In his precritical writings, Kant definitely held that there is such a real opposition between realities. In the essay on negative quantities, in fact, he treats this opposition as a general "conservation law," guaranteeing that "the sum of all existing reality insofar as it is grounded in the world is, regarded in itself, equal to zero."[48] He hastens to add, however, that this does not "cancel" the positive reality of the world because the world is not wholly negative in relation to its ground (the divine will) but possesses positive reality in relation to it. The reality of the world is only "equal to zero" when the "inner real grounds" of its finite constituents are considered in relation to one another. Yet in the *Beweisgrund* essay of the same year, Kant does appear to draw the conclusion that the real opposition between realities precludes the existence of an *ens realissimum* in the strict sense. For he denies that the "sum of realities" can belong to God "as determinations occurring beside one another in a single subject," since in that case a *Realrepugnanz* would occur between them. The divine nature, he insists, "contains the highest real-

48. *Gesammelte Schriften*, 2:197; cf. England, *Kant's Conception of God*, p. 69.

ity" only in the sense that it is the wholly simple and necessarily existent "final real ground" of the realities in all other things.[49]

There can be no doubt that in the *Lectures on Philosophical Theology* and the *Critique of Pure Reason* Kant does conceive of God as an *ens realissimum*, a being possessing as its determinations all the realities found in all possible things. To those such as England and Kemp Smith who take a Kantian doctrine to be "critical" in proportion as it involves a rejection of the metaphysics of Kant's rationalist predecessors, this shift must remain a bewildering reversion to a rationalistic standpoint which Kant had surpassed already in the early sixties. Yet in fact it was precisely Kant's critical doctrines, and particularly his distinction between phenomenal and noumenal reality, which made it possible for him to accept the concept of God as an *en realissimum*. In the Amphiboly, Kant asserts that "real conflict does take place everywhere, so that A − B = 0: that is, one reality combined with another in the same subject cancels its effect."[50] But he explicitly restricts the knowable instances of this conflict to the "obstacles and counteracting effects in nature . . . which . . . must be called *realitates phaenomena*." So in keeping with his critical doctrines, Kant adopts a strictly agnostic position on the question whether *realitates noumena*, the pure realities which might constitute the divine nature, can also conflict in this way. As Kant makes clear in the *Lectures on Philosophical Theology*, neither the real possibility nor the real impossibility of an *ens realissimum* can be demonstrated.[51] It is to strictly *precritical* doctrines, therefore, that England and Kemp Smith are appealing when they argue that Kant's ontology commits him to the real impossibility of uniting all realities in one individual thing.

Assessment of Kant's Theory

Kant himself realized that his readers might easily be put off by the Dialectic's pretensions to a systematic and exhaustive

49. *Gesammelte Schriften*, 2:85–86.
50. *Critique of Pure Reason*, A 273/B 329.
51. *Critique of Pure Reason*, A 264/B 320: "If reality is represented only through the pure understanding (as *realitas noumenon*), then no conflict can be thought between realities, i.e., no relation like that between things which cancel each other in their consequences when combined in one subject."

account of the workings of human reason in general.[52] And in this particular case, it is not hard for many of us to regard Kant's account of the rational origin of the idea of an *ens realissimum* and his argument for its rational indispensability as highly artificial and farfetched. It certainly seems that the idea of the divine, and even of a single supreme Deity, not only historically antedates but seems in itself far easier to understand and accept than the abstruse metaphysical doctrines from which Kant pretends to derive it. Kant's theory, moreover, is prima facie most counterintuitive. It is difficult to find any spiritual affinity between dry reasoning about thorough determination in the abstract and the religious attitudes with which the idea of God might naturally be associated.

To begin with, the fact must be faced squarely that Kant's principal interest in the concept of God is not motivated by any concern with revealed theology, empirical anthropology, or comparative religions. Kant's God is, most aggressively, the God of the philosophers. And as an Enlightenment philosopher, Kant shares the Enlightenment's suspicion of all revealed or ecclesiastical religions and all popular religious cults. These he views as sources of superstition, religious fanaticism, and a moral authoritarianism which is subversive of rationality and human dignity.[53] If Kant occasionally uses his rational theology to interpret the doctrines or religious symbols of popular cults, this is only because he believes that these cults have not altogether failed to perform their proper function of inspiring in the hearts of men a respect for the moral law and the attitudes of rational faith and reverence which go with it. Their deities resemble the God of rational theology, because they are images, albeit often crude and distorted ones, of this God.

Gesammelte Schriften, 28, 2, 2, pp. 1023–1027; *Lectures on Philosophical Theology*, pp. 54–58.

52. *Critique of Pure Reason*, A xiv: "In this business I have made exhaustiveness my chief aim in view, and I am bold to say that there is not a single metaphysical problem which is not here resolved, or at least the key to which has not been supplied. . . . I believe, while I am saying this, that I perceive on the face of my reader an expression of indignation, mixed with contempt, at claims so pretentious and immodest."

53. *Gesammelte Schriften*, 28, 2, 2, pp. 1002, 1118; *Lectures on Philosophical Theology*, pp. 31, 160f.

The chief objection to Kant's theory, however, is not that it is philosophy, but that it is bad philosophy, a contrived piece of baroque metaphysics borrowed from eighteenth-century German scholasticism, and devoid of any deeper interest or significance. This is what Kemp Smith has in mind when he dismisses Section 2 of the Ideal of Pure Reason as "quite the most archaic piece of rationalistic argument in the entire *Critique*. It is not merely Leibnizian but Wolffian in character. . . . [Kant] is here, as it were, recalling, not altogether without sympathy, the lessons of his student years." [54] And the only positive value Kemp Smith can see in Kant's rehearsing of these outdated views is that "they enable him to render definite, by way of contrast, the outcome of his own Critical teaching."

No one, I believe, would wish to argue that Kant's theory of the rational ideal is a profoundly original or revolutionary part of the critical philosophy. But Kemp Smith's account of it here, it seems to me, does involve a serious misestimate of it in several respects. First, Kemp Smith implies that this theory is at odds with Kant's critical views. We have just seen that there is no basis to the charge that the Ideal of Pure Reason ignores critical doctrines about real opposition between realities, as expressed in the Amphiboly. But we have also seen that Kant's account of the origin of the idea of God, despite the many Leibnizian elements present in it, carefully reinterprets these Leibnizian doctrines so that they dovetail with the critical philosophy. Kant's theory is based on his own version of the traditional ontology, as set forth in the Kantian categories of quality and their application in the Schematism and the Anticipations of Perception. It is also based on Kant's version of the Leibnizian notion of absolute possibility, as it is adumbrated in the Postulates of Empirical Thought. At least some of what may strike us as scholastic subtlety in Kant's presentation must be attributed to the fact that he is attempting to work out these Leibnizian ideas in a genuinely critical context, keeping clearly in mind the distinctions between understanding and sense, pure and empirical thought, analysis and synthesis, logical, real, and absolute possibility.

We must also be careful to bring to Kant's theory of the ra-

54. *Commentary*, p. 522.

tional origin of the idea of God a realistic conception of what his project is. An attempt to identify the rational origin and demonstrate the rational inevitability of the idea of God is not an attempt to do religious anthropology a priori, nor is it an attempt to describe the psychological process by which anyone in fact comes to have this idea. Instead, it is an attempt to show how the concept of a supremely real being arises naturally and even inevitably in the course of working out the implications of a set of commonly accepted metaphysical presuppositions. We could say that the project is not one of describing how people in fact come to have a concept of God, but rather of showing why anyone who thinks philosophically had better have it. Of course any such project has to be carried on relative to a particular set of metaphysical presuppositions, and some metaphysical theories doubtless lack any materials out of which an argument for the rational inevitability of the idea of God could be constructed. The point to be made is just that Kant's metaphysics does not lack them, as Kant himself saw very clearly.

When Kemp Smith describes Kant's theory as "not merely Leibnizian, but Wolffian in character," his main purpose is to stigmatize it as arid and uninteresting by associating it with the less profound and original of Kant's rationalist precursors. Literally speaking, however, the remark is just inaccurate. Hints of Kant's line of thought can be found in some of the manuscripts of Leibniz, but nothing even close to it is to be found either in Wolff or in Baumgarten. Wolff's only account of the origin of our idea of God is in fact merely an unimaginative restatement of the Cartesian argument we discussed earlier. No one prior to Kant seems to have argued explicitly that the idea of God takes its rational origin from the fact that it is presupposed by any attempt to think of individual things in general as thoroughly determined, and hence as absolutely possible. For better or worse, the Kantian theory is original with Kant.

But of course this is not to say that Kant was the first philosopher to argue for the view that our concepts of finite things somehow imply or presuppose the idea of God. Kemp Smith is quite correct in calling Kant's theory of the origin of this idea "archaic" if by that term we mean that it belongs to a long tradition of philosophical thinking. It belongs to the mainstream of Western theology and metaphysics to think that imperfect things can serve to remind the human intellect of a perfect being who is their first cause, and that the idea of this being has a kind of priority in the order of concepts corresponding to the causal priority in the order of things which belongs to its divine object. We have seen that different versions of this view can be found in Descartes, Leibniz, and Wolff, and it could equally have been found in Spinoza and Malebranche. Earlier statements of similar views are plentiful in the Scholastic tradition. Says St. Augustine: "I saw that all finite things are in you, not as though you were a place, but because you hold all things in the hand of your truth, and all things are true insofar as they are." St. Thomas Aquinas calls God the "universally perfect being" who serves as the "common measure" of all things. And St. Bonaventure hints very strongly at both the Cartesian and the Kantian arguments for the rational necessity of the idea of an *ens realissimum*. In *The Mind's Road to God*, he cites Averroes' principle that "privations and defects can in no way be known except through position" and goes on to conclude from this that "our intellect is not able to reach a fully resolved understanding of any created being unless it is supported by the understanding of the most pure, actual, complete and absolute Being."[55]

Kant's theory in Section 2 of the Ideal of Pure Reason thus stands deeply rooted in a long tradition of philosophical and religious thought. It develops this tradition by filling out Descartes' argument for the rational necessity of the idea of God through the use of Leibniz's conception of absolute possibility and its relation to Leibnizian complete individual notions. And it does all this carefully within the confines of Kant's own authentically critical views. It may be, of course, that the entire tradition at this point is telling only "an unconvincing tale." Even so, Kant's version of it would have to be accounted one of its most sophisticated and thoughtful redactions.

55. St. Augustine, *Opera, Patrologia Latina*, ed. J. P. Migne (Paris, 1861), p. 32, c. 744; cf. *Confessions*, 8, 15 (Baltimore, 1961), p. 150. St. Thomas Aquinas, *Summa Contra Gentiles*, Leonine edition (Lyons, 1950) 1, 28, 8. St. Bonaventure, *Opera Omnia* (Quaracchi, 1891), 5:304; cf. *Works* (Paterson, N.J., 1960), 1:30.

The Ground of All Possibility

Kant's Proof for God's Existence

Kant describes God as an *ens logice originarium* because, viewed in terms of an ideal process of thorough determination, every individual concept is derived from the concept of God, while this concept alone is "original" and completely underivative. But Kant also speaks of God simply as the *ens originarium*, as if he were the ground or cause of things themselves. As we just noted, in Kant's scholastic and rationalist predecessors the two sorts of "originality" were closely associated. They held that there is an intimate connection between the rational or logical order among concepts and the causal order among things. Nothing, they maintained, is without a sufficient ground or reason for its being as it is and not otherwise, and this ground ultimately lies in some concept from which the concept of the thing can be derived.[56] Hence the underivative status of the concept of God and its priority to all other concepts was for them very closely bound up with the preeminent ontological and causal status of God himself. Because this concept is the only one which can be formed entirely "through itself," God alone contains in himself his own ground or reason, and thus he alone exists independently and necessarily. In a like manner, the fact that the concepts of other things are thought through the concept of the supremely real being means that their existence is causally dependent on God's. The unique status of the concept

---

56. Spinoza held that God is "conceived through himself" and also that "without God nothing can be, or be conceived" (*Ethics*, 1, a. 88, and p. xv). Along these same lines, Leibniz in an early manuscript insists that "whatever is thought by us is either conceived in itself or involves the concept of something else," and by rejecting the possibility of an infinite regress he infers from this that "if nothing is conceived through itself, nothing at all will be conceived." He goes on to conjecture that "there is only one thing which is conceived through itself, namely God himself, and next to this only nothing or privation." Ideally, therefore, he says, all things may be "analyzed into God and nothing" just as in the binary system all numbers may be expressed as combinations of zero and one. L. Couturat, ed., *Opuscules et fragments inedits de Leibniz* (Paris, 1903), pp. 429–431. Cf. *Philosophical Writings*, pp. 1–3.

of God, in short, was closely bound up with both the ontological and cosmological arguments for his existence.

Kant's divergence from this general line of thought appears as early as his Latin essay *Nova dilucidatio* of 1755. Here Kant rejects the Wolffian principle that an entity can contain in itself the ground of its own existence, and unites this with a criticism of the ontological argument.[57] More detailed and more characteristically Kantian criticisms of the ontological and cosmological arguments are advanced eight years later in Kant's important essay *Der einzig mögliche Beweisgrund zu einer Demonstration des Daseins Gottes* (1763) (*The Only Possible Ground of Proof for a Demonstration of God's Existence*). The *Beweisgrund* essay begins with a rejection of the ontological argument, and of the concept of necessary existence involved in it. Being or existence, Kant insists, is not a "reality" and therefore cannot make up the content of any predicate or be included in the concept of any subject. Rather, it is the absolute "positing" (*Position, Setzung*) of an object corresponding to a concept. There can be nothing, therefore, whose nonexistence can be self-contradictory, and whose existence is, in this sense, necessary. Kant then proceeds to reject the Wolffian version of the cosmological argument because, he contends, it presupposes this same illegitimate concept of logically necessary existence, and thus rests on the same error as the ontological proof.[58] Kant's criticisms of the traditional proofs in the *Beweisgrund* essay are thus essentially the same as his more famous attacks on transcendental theology in the *Critique of Pure Reason* almost twenty years later.

The *Beweisgrund* essay, however, is far from a rejection of transcendental theology. On the contrary, it contains not only an a priori demonstration of God's existence, but a defense of the concept of necessary existence, and an attempt to connect

57. Kant's objection to Wolff at this point is the same as Arnauld's objection to Descartes on the same issue: God cannot contain his own *ratio essendi* or be a *causa sui* since every ground or cause is "prior to" what it grounds or effects, and nothing can be prior to itself. *Gesammelte Schriften*, 1:394–5; cf. England, *Kant's Conception of God*, pp. 223–224. Cf. Descartes, *Oeuvres*, 7:208ff; *Philosophical Works*, 2:88ff.

58. *Gesammelte Schriften*, 2:72–75, 158.

the "logical originality" of the concept of God with the ontological priority of the supreme being as the ground of all other
things. The object of Kant's attack in the essay is only a certain
conception of necessary existence, and the theistic proofs employing this erroneous conception. His real aim is to work out
a more defensible conception and to show how it may be employed to better advantage in theistic arguments.

The *Beweisgrund* proof, which had been presented earlier in
the *Nova dilucidatio*, attempts to show that the existence of an *ens
realissimum* is necessary because it is a condition for all possibility in general. (For the sake of a convenient terminology, I will
call it the "possibility proof.")[59]

Kant begins his proof by distinguishing between two kinds of
impossibility. A supposition, he says, is "formally" impossible
when its concept is unthinkable because it contains a contradiction. It is "materially" impossible, however, when it is unthinkable because "no material, no *datum* is there to think." As we
have already noted, all possibility for Kant consists in thinkability, in the relation between the possible entity or state of
affairs and some faculty of the mind which enables the mind to
form a concept of the possibility in question. To think a possibility for Kant is to form a concept whose "material" or content
consists in certain realities (or their negations). For a certain concept to be thinkable, therefore, the realities in question must be
somehow available to the mind which is to think them. Kant
maintains, however, that for a reality to be thus available for
thought it must be "given" to the intellect through some actually
existing thing in which it is to be found.

From these considerations, Kant concludes that "it is absolutely impossible that nothing at all should exist." For if nothing
at all existed, then no realities could be "given" as the material
for any thought. Hence nothing would be thinkable, and hence
nothing would be possible. "To be sure," Kant concedes, "there

59. In one of his reflections, Kant calls it the "transcendental proof." (Refl.
5522, *Gesammelte Schriften*, 18:206. This term, however, was also used occasionally for the ontological argument (cf. Refl. 6027, ibid., p. 427) and Kant
seems to have applied it generally to any argument which attempts to establish God's existence wholly a priori, without any appeal whatever to experience
(cf. *Critique of Pure Reason*, A 591/B 619).

is no inner contradiction in the denial of all existence." But the supposition that nothing exists is nevertheless impossible. For any supposition "through which all possibility in general is canceled, is absolutely impossible." [60] The supposition that nothing exists, however, is according to Kant's reasoning, a supposition of just this sort.

Kant now goes on to infer the existence of a necessary being. He says: "All possibility presupposes something actual in which and through which everything thinkable is given. Hence there is a certain actuality, the canceling of which would cancel all inner possibility in general. But that whose canceling or denial does away with all possibility is absolutely necessary. Hence something exists in an absolutely necessary manner." [61] Kant then proceeds to infer that the being which has this necessary mode of existence must be one being rather than many, must be eternal and immutable, must have understanding and will: in short, that it must be a God. [62]

Kant's possibility proof for God's existence is open to question at several points. Perhaps the strangest claim in it, at least at first glance, is that for a reality to be an object of thought it must be instantiated somewhere in an existing thing. In fact, however, this is only an unfamiliar (and precritical) version of one of the critical philosophy's most empiricist doctrines. As we saw above, every concept for Kant requires both a form, supplied by the understanding, and a content, given in sensible intuition. [63] Concepts lacking in such content are "empty" or "problematic" concepts, concepts *ohne Sinn und Bedeutung*, and through them nothing can be known or even known to have real (as opposed to mere logical) possibility. It is a version of this requirement of a "datum for what is thinkable" which Kant was expressing in his possibility proof. Of course, there is nothing here suggesting that such "data" must be given through the faculty of sensibility: indeed, if they must be given through the supreme reality of a necessarily existing Deity, it is evident that they need not be

60. *Gesammelte Schriften*, 2:78–79.
61. Ibid., p. 83.
62. Ibid., pp. 83–89.
63. *Critique of Pure Reason*, A 239/B 298.

given through any being of sense. But it was not until the *Inaugural Dissertation* of 1770 that Kant began to relate the two necessary elements of the thinkable respectively to the active and passive faculty of the mind, understanding and sense. It is only the distinction of the formal and material elements themselves which concern him in the *Beweisgrund* essay.

The possibility proof, however, certainly does depend very heavily on Kant's identification of possibility with thinkability, and perhaps on an illegitimate form of it. In the case where a concept is "unthinkable" because it is incoherent, it does seem to follow that it is impossible for there to be anything answering to it. But the conclusion is not nearly so evident when the "unthinkability" is founded on a mere absence of data for thought. A completely empty world would indeed be one in which nothing is thinkable; for such a world would be lacking not only in data for thought, but also in minds to think any data. But it does not seem to follow from this alone that nothing *could have* existed, so that any empty world is eo ipso a *necessarily* empty world. What Kant's thoroughgoing identification of possibility with thinkability appears to involve here is an exclusion out of hand of the prima facie possibility that the world might have been empty simply because nothing happened to exist in it.

Given the Kantian account of modal concepts, in fact, there are some grounds for holding that Kant's inference from the emptiness of a world to its necessary emptiness (to the impossibility of anything's existing) is strictly illegitimate. For the reason that Kant is entitled to the conclusion that nothing is possible in an empty world is that the concept of possibility is inapplicable there, depending as it does on the relation of some mind or mental faculty to its representations. But in a totally empty world, the same considerations seem to render all other modal concepts (in particular, necessity and impossibility) equally inapplicable, since in such a world there would be no minds and no representations of any kind for them to contemplate.

Kant, however, is concerned in his argument not with the fact that an empty world would be empty of minds, but with the fact that it would be empty of the material components or data necessary to the formation of concepts which might apply to objects. He seems in fact more or less to suppose that the completely empty world is being contemplated by a mind, which is able to judge the impossibility of anything's existing by noting the absence of data for thought. Perhaps Kant is imagining the totally empty world to be contemplated by a purely hypothetical mind, or again perhaps by our actual minds, as a merely hypothetical world. But once we allow the empty world to be contemplated by a mind, by considering that world as merely hypothetical or by introducing what is purely hypothetical in relation to that world, what is to prevent us from importing the requisite material components of possibility into our empty world by similar devices? Kant is playing a very deep game here, and it is hard to say what fair rules for this game would look like.

Leibniz and Wolff both held that for something to be possible is for it to be thought by the divine intellect.[64] This idea seems to be what lies behind Kant's unqualified identification of the possible with the thinkable, and the impossible with the unthinkable. But such identifications are less problematic when they presuppose the all-knowing intellect of a supremely perfect being who must exist in every possible world, than in their Kantian version where no such presupposition can be counted upon, and where we must face the bewildering prospect of applying these criteria for possibility and impossibility in worlds where there is supposed to be no such intellect, where there is supposed to be nothing at all.

Again, Kant might be accused of trading on an ambiguity when he argues that a supposition through which "all possibility in general is canceled" must itself be "absolutely impossible." This claim is easy enough to accept if "all possibility" means something like "all possible states of affairs." But in the Kantian argument "all possibility" must instead refer to something on the order of "all possible *things*." For the argument thus far has been that a completely empty world would be one in which all particular things would be impossible, because none of the realities needed to think them would be present as data

64. Leibniz, *Philosophische Schriften*, 6:614; cf. *Philosophical Writings*, p. 185. Wolff, *Metaphysik*, §975, pp. 601f.

for the corresponding thoughts. But even granting this argument, it looks as if one possible state of affairs might be that in which nothing exists (and, thus, according to the argument, in which nothing is possible). The canceling of all possible things does not obviously involve the canceling of all possible alternative states of affairs unless it is shown that an empty (and thus, on the argument, a necessarily empty) world is not a possible state of affairs.

On Kant's behalf it might be replied that the actual existence of things suffices to show it impossible that there should be a *necessarily* empty world. Indeed, even the premise "possibly something exists" would suffice, given Kant's argument up to this point, to show that "something exists" is a necessary truth.[65] The possibility proof may therefore not be quite so vulnerable at this point as it first appears.

Perhaps the most clearly indefensible step in Kant's argument, however, is the next one, which moves from "necessarily something exists" to "something exists in an absolutely necessary manner." Kant may have shown that the world is necessarily nonempty, that there have to be things in it. But this does not justify the conclusion that this necessity must, so to speak, take up residence in some particular thing. There is no contradiction in supposing that a necessarily nonempty world should be one composed entirely of things whose particular existence

---

65. Let p stand for the proposition that something exists. Then the proof goes as follows:

(1) $Mp \ni p$		Kant's argument
(2) $Mp \supset LMp$		axiom
(3) $p \ni Mp$		axiom
(4) $p \equiv Mp$		1, 3
(5) $(Lq \ \& \ (q \equiv r)) \supset Lr$		theorem
(6) Mp		hypothesis
(7) LMp		2, 6
(8) $LMp \ \& \ (Mp \equiv p)$		4, 7
(9) Lp		5, 8

(1) has (presumably) already been established by Kant's argument that every possibility presupposes something existing. (2) and (3) are standard axioms of modal logic. ((3) is the contrapositive of Lewis and Langford's A7 and (2) is a version of their C11 in the system S5). (See C. I. Lewis and C. H. Langford, *Symbolic Logic* (New York, 1959), pp. 493, 497.) (5) is a theorem of modal logic. Given these premises and the hypothesis (6), (9) follows.

is contingent. Kant is led to draw the inference, no doubt, because he already has in mind the notion of a being whose existence would *eo ipso* guarantee the possibility of all beings, whatever the constitution of their realities and negations may be. Since God's being fills the whole of "ontological space," his necessary existence would at once safeguard the possibility of everything else. Relying on this, Kant found it easy in the passage quoted above to pass from "all possibility presupposes something actual" to "there is a certain actuality, the canceling of which would cancel all possibility in general." But the inference is still a fallacious one.[66]

The Possibility Proof in the Critical Writings.

Given the shakiness of Kant's possibility proof for God's existence, it is not surprising that he ceased to support it in his critical works. What is more remarkable is that he never wholly repudiated this proof, and that the line of argument contained in it continued to shape his thought about natural theology throughout his later writings. In both the *Lectures on Philosophical Theology* and the first critique, Kant insists that there are only three theistic proofs, the ontological, the cosmological, and the physicotheological. The *Lectures* discuss the possibility proof not under the heading of a theistic argument, but as an argument for the claim that "the *ens realissimum* must be the *ens entium*."[67] In the *Critique*, the possibility proof appears chiefly in the context of Kant's account of the manner in which reason arrives at the concept of God.

In Kant's critical thought, therefore, the possibility proof leads

---

66. Kant was not, however, the first to commit such a fallacy in the course of a theistic argument. Locke argues that since "we know there is some real being, and that nonentity cannot produce any real being, it is an evident demonstration that *from eternity there has been something*. . . . And that eternal Being must be most powerful*" (Locke, *Essay concerning Human Understanding*, ed. Peter H. Nidditch (Oxford, 1975) Book IV, ch. X, sec. 3–4). Locke's premises justify the conclusion that from eternity there has always been something just as Kant's argument (perhaps) shows that "something exists" is a necessary truth. But just as Kant is not justified in concluding from this that there is a necessary being, so Locke is not justified in concluding that there is an eternal one.

67. *Gesammelte Schriften*, 28, 2, 2, pp. 1033f; *Lectures on Philosophical Theology*, pp. 65f.

a rather shadowy life. But its presence there is nevertheless undeniable. In the *Lectures*, Kant describes God as "the root of all possibility," and speaks in other ways strongly suggestive of the possibility proof. Referring explicitly to the *Beweisgrund* essay, Kant says that the theistic proof contained in it "can in no way be refuted, because it has its ground in the nature of human reason." "*Realiter*," he tells us, "we have no concept of possibility except through existence, and in the case of every possibility which we think *realiter* we always presuppose some existence; if not the actuality of the thing itself, then at least an actuality in general containing the data for everything possible."[68]

Nowhere in the *Critique* is the possibility proof set forth so explicitly. In the Ideal of Pure Reason, however, considerations drawn from it are used to support Kant's derivation of the ideal of pure reason from the complete determination of things. The two lines of thought certainly have a good deal of affinity with one another and are easily run together:

> Thus all possibility of things (the synthesis of the manifold, according to its content) is to be regarded as derivative, and only the possibility of that which includes all reality in itself is to be regarded as original. For all negations . . . are mere limitations of a greater and finally of the highest reality, and so they presuppose it, and are derived from it according to their content.[69]

The presence of the possibility proof in this passage is unmistakable. Yet to a reader unfamiliar with Kant's more detailed statements of this proof in the *Lectures* or in his precritical writings, it would surely be difficult to see what he is driving at here. Surely much of the obscurity of the Ideal of Pure Reason is due to the constant presence, usually just below the surface, of a subtle line of thinking which is nowhere made quite explicit. And much of the impression of metaphysical artificiality and "Wolffian" rationalism is surely also to be explained by the fact that Kant's main argument is tangled up with ideas derived from the possibility proof.

68. *Gesammelte Schriften*, 28, 2, 2, p. 1036; *Lectures on Philosophical Theology*, p. 68.

69. *Critique of Pure Reason*, A 578/B 606.

But exactly what was Kant's attitude toward this proof in his critical period? The passages quoted above, and particularly the one drawn from the *Lectures*, might seem to endorse the proof almost without qualification. Kant emphatically denies, however, that the possibility proof succeeds in demonstrating God's existence. Shortly after the passage just quoted from the *Critique*, he hastens to add that "all this does not signify the objective relation of an actual object to other things, but only of the *idea to concepts*." "It is self-evident," he insists, "that reason in respect to its aim of representing the thorough determination of things does not presuppose the existence of a being which measures up to the ideal, but only its idea."[70] In the *Lectures*, however, while conceding that the possibility proof is "unable to establish the objective necessity of an original being," nevertheless does credit it with showing "the subjective necessity of such a being," and demonstrating that God's existence is a "necessary presupposition" or "necessary hypothesis" of human reason.[71] Kant provides a bit more explanation of this language when he says: "That is, our speculative reason sees that it is necessary to presuppose this being if it wants to have insight into *why* something is possible." And again: "My reason makes it absolutely necessary for me to assume a being which is the ground of everything possible, because otherwise I would be unable to know what in general the possibility of something consists in."[72]

Kant's meaning in these passages is hardly transparent, but perhaps his idea is something along the following lines: Empirical real possibility is the agreement of some concept "with the formal conditions of experience," that is, with the mathematical principles governing space and time, and the a priori laws of synthesis which constitute the form of an empirical object in general. But this does not explain to us the possibility of a thing

70. *Critique of Pure Reason*, A 577–79/B 605–07.
71. *Gesammelte Schriften*, 28, 2, 2, p. 1036; *Lectures on Philosophical Theology*, p. 68. That these were views Kant still held in his critical period further confirmed by a number of his reflections (see Refl. 5492, 5502, 5508, 5522, 5525, *Gesammelte Schriften*, 18, pp. 197, 201, 203, 207, 208.)
72. *Gesammelte Schriften*, 28, 2, 2, p. 1036; *Lectures on Philosophical Theology*, p. 68.

in general, its "absolute possibility" irrespective of its relation
to our experience. The only such concept we have is the conformity of the object to the conditions of pure understanding,
that is, of "thinkability" in general. These conditions, as we
have already seen, involve both the noncontradictoriness of the
form of the concept through which the thing is thought, and
also the "givenness" of the realities which go to make up the
content or intension of that concept. Where the question is not
the possibility of some specific thing, but rather of any and all
particular things considered generally, the latter condition is
satisfied most comprehensively, systematically, and economi-
cally by the "assumption" or "hypothesis" of an *ens realissimum*,
with whose existence the whole of ontological space at once is
"given."

The appeal of this "hypothesis" is purely "subjective" in at
least two ways. In the first place, there is no positive reason at
all to think that the actuality presupposed by the absolute possibility of things in general is a necessarily existent *ens realissimum*. There are any number of ways in which the necessary
realities might all be given in finite beings. But the *ens realissimum* "hypothesis" appeals to our reason's taste for simplicity
and completeness; it is the most natural way in which reason
can give a systematic account of the material conditions of all
possibility. Hence we quite naturally tend to "assume" it as the
most satisfying explanation for possibility in general.

The assumption is also purely "subjective" in that it rests on
the complete identification of possibility with "thinkability,"
and indeed with the latter conceived in a manner rather analogous to our own sensibly conditioned power of thought. This
may perhaps be (for Kant, it certainly is) the only manner in
which we can form any definite notion of the possibility of
things in general. But this does not mean that absolute real possibility might not, in itself, have some quite different foundation.

That views something like these were held by Kant, can be
seen from what is said in the *Critique*. Section 2 of the Ideal of
Pure Reason concludes with an account of the "natural illusion
of reason" in relation to the idea of a supreme being. Again, the
precritical writings are nowhere mentioned explicitly. But it is

evident even from the terms in which Kant poses his problem that he has the possibility proof in mind. It is equally clear, once we are familiar with the possibility proof in its more explicit form, that in the *Critique* Kant still regards this proof as having a kind of natural appeal to human reason, and that he is trying in this chapter to account on critical principles for the hold this proof still has on him. "How," he asks, "does reason come to regard all possibility of things as derived from a single possibility as its foundation, namely, that of a highest reality, and to presuppose this reality as contained in one particular original being?"

"The answer," he tells us, "is evident from the results of the transcendental analytic. The possibility of objects of sense is their relation to our thought." The "matter" of this thought, says Kant, "must be given, since without that it cannot be thought at all, and thus its possibility cannot be represented." Further, he argues, the real in experience which provides our concepts with their content is subject to the synthetic unity of apperception, through which it "is a single, all-embracing experience." Consequently, "the material for the possibility of all objects of sense must be presupposed as given in one sum (*Inbegriff*)." "Nothing," therefore, "is *for us* an object unless it presupposes the sum of all empirical reality as a condition of its possibility."

When we try to form a concept of the absolute possibility of things, irrespective of the sensible conditions of our experience, we naturally rely on this fundamental principle of thinkability under these conditions, and attempt to apply the same principle of synthetic unity to the thinkability (and hence the possibility) of things in general. By a "natural illusion," says Kant, "we hold the empirical principle of our concept of the possibility of things to be a transcendental principle of the possibility of things in general." And this leads us to "hypostatize" the idea of a "sum of all reality" and treat it as an individual thing, whose necessary existence provides the ground for all possibility.[73]

Just how satisfactory is Kant's final resolution of the possibil-

---

73. *Critique of Pure Reason*, A 581f/B 609f.

ity proof? Kant might have simply rejected this proof, for any of several good reasons (though the force of at least some of the objections to it would undoubtedly be dampened considerably if the proof is taken to establish only a "subjectively necessary hypothesis" rather than a "dogmatic conclusion"). But in fact Kant seems never to have repudiated the possibility proof. He seems always to have taken seriously the thoroughgoing identification of possibility and thinkability which the proof presupposes, and the associated idea that every possibility presupposes some actuality. Moreover, he seems always to have found it natural to draw from these considerations the conclusion that there must exist an *ens realissimum* serving as the "substratum for all possibility."

In the *Critique*, this conclusion is described as a "dialectical illusion," arising, like the others treated in the Dialectic, from our reason's inevitable but misleading tendency to apply to things in themselves an a priori principle valid only for appearances. In this case it is the principle that all possibility presupposes a material substratum, given in one whole, which is thus misapplied. There is certainly ground to wonder whether it is really so natural to apply such a principle as it is applied in the possibility proof, but at least in the *Critique* this proof is dismissed as an illusion. More disturbing is Kant's more complex and more sympathetic handling of the possibility proof in the *Lectures on Philosophical Theology*. Here Kant claims that the proof is "subjectively" valid, because the existence of an *ens realissimum* is the only way in which we can conceive of a ground for the possibility of things in general. On the other hand, he denies "objective" validity to the proof, apparently because he regards it as failing to show that the possibility of things really has to be grounded in just this way.

But is such a distinction between "subjective" and "objective" validity really defensible? Let us suppose it to be the case that the only way in which we can conceive of the action of gravitational force is to suppose that bodies act on one another at a distance. Of course we do not know how gravitational attraction works, nor have we any way of finally excluding the possibility that gravitation works by some means other than action at a distance (a means of which, by hypothesis, we can form no clear notion at all). Even so, I submit, we would be justified under these circumstances in supposing it quite likely that bodies do indeed ("objectively") act on one another at a distance. For the hypothesis of action at a distance does explain the data, and (as we have supposed) it is the only hypothesis available to us which does. Now that hypothesis which provides the best available explanation of a set of data tends to be confirmed by that set of data. On our supposition, therefore, gravitational phenomena tend to confirm the hypothesis of action at a distance.

In a like manner, if it is really true that the existence of a most real being is the only hypothesis by which we can account for the absolute possibility of things in general, then the existence of such possibilities must count as evidence confirming that hypothesis. Kant himself seems to drift in this direction when he says that the possibility proof shows us that God's existence is a "necessary hypothesis" without proving "with apodictic certainty" that God exists.[74] For although a set of data provides evidence in favor of that hypothesis which counts as its only available explanation, such data obviously do not provide an

---

74. *Gesammelte Schriften*, 28, 2, 2, p. 1034; *Lectures on Philosophical Theology*, p. 66. In the *Critique*, Kant seems to endorse, in a qualified way, a parallel line of reasoning in his discussion of both the cosmological and teleological proofs. At one point he grants, for the sake of argument, that the existence of a necessary being can be demonstrated from the supposition of something contingently existing. He then notes that the "logical originality" of the *ens realissimum* "fulfills, at least in one part, the concept of unconditioned necessity." "It," says Kant, "it is a question of a *decision*, that is, if the existence of some necessary being is conceded, and if it is further agreed that we must take up the question where this necessity is to be posited, then it cannot be denied that there is a certain foundation for this concept; for then one cannot choose better, or rather, one has no choice at all, but is required to give his voice to the absolute unity of complete reality as the original source of possibility." Kant avoids the conclusion only by insisting that after all "nothing impels us to decide," since our purpose is "merely to judge how much we can really know about this subject" (*Critique of Pure Reason*, A 587/B 615). He reasons similarly regarding the teleological argument: "Yet it must be admitted that if we should specify a cause" for the order observable in nature, "we cannot proceed more securely than by analogy with those purposive productions whose causes and mode of operation are alone fully known to us. Reason could never answer for itself if it left behind a causality with which it is acquainted in favor of obscure and unprovable grounds of explanation with which it is not acquainted" (*Critique of Pure Reason*, A 626/B 655).

apodictic demonstration of the truth of this hypothesis. Even when the "datum" itself is something a priori, such as the bare possibility of things in general, it still seems in a case like this to be only a question of preponderant evidence, and not one of strict proof.

Such a view of the possibility proof would run counter to Kant's usual critical attitude toward metaphysical questions. Kant often insists that such questions, if they can be decided at all, have to be decided a priori and with apodictic certainty; hypotheses, conjectures, and merely probable opinions on them are ruled out.[75] Yet Kant is also sometimes inclined to think of theoretical arguments for God's existence, despite their inconclusiveness, as somehow pointing the way toward practical faith. This tendency lies behind his extremely sympathetic treatment of the physicotheological argument both in the *Critique* and in the *Lectures on Philosophical Theology*. And there is even a strong suggestion in the *Critique* that the same is true of the cosmological argument.[76] It seems likely, therefore, from what is said in the *Lectures* that Kant was also occasionally inclined during his critical period to treat the possibility proof with a like sympathy. Indeed, he even goes so far as to credit it with being "the one of all possible proofs which affords the most satisfaction."[77]

The possibility proof was originally an outgrowth of Kant's attempt to preserve the concept of necessary existence, despite

75. "In this species of investigation it is in no way allowed to hold *opinions*. Everything which looks like a hypothesis is a forbidden commodity; it should not be put up for sale even for the lowest price, but should be confiscated as soon as it is discovered" (*Critique of Pure Reason*, A xiv).

76. "Nevertheless, this argument retains a certain importance, and a regard which we cannot take from it, merely on account of its objective insufficiency. For granted that there are obligations in the idea of reason which are wholly correct but which in application to us would be lacking in any reality . . . if a highest being were not presupposed; then we would even be under an obligation to follow those concepts which, although they may not be objectively sufficient, are still preponderant according to the standard of our reason. . . . The duty to choose would thus throw the indecision of speculation out of balance by a practical addition" (*Critique of Pure Reason*, A 588f/B 616f).

77. *Gesammelte Schriften*, 28, 2, 2, p. 1034; *Lectures on Philosophical Theology*, p. 66.

the strictures concerning the ontological and cosmological arguments with which his name is closely associated. We might like to think that so tortuous and dubious an argument could be entirely relegated to the category of those "precritical" views to which a student of the mature Kant need pay no attention. Unfortunately, however, Kant will not let us do this. The possibility proof, as we have seen, is an extension of the Kantian account of the origin of the idea of God, and one which Kant incorporated into his account of the "natural illusion" of reason with regard to its ideal. The *Lectures* reveal an even greater sympathy with the proof. Thus whatever faults we may find with it, we must face the fact that the possibility proof always retained such an appeal for Kant himself that his critical thought on the subject of rational theology cannot be properly understood without an appreciation of its influence.

The Divine Attributes

In the *Lectures on Philosophical Theology*, Kant says that the concept of God is the most "precisely determined" of all our concepts.[78] But he is referring here primarily to the special place occupied by this concept in an ideal procedure for the "complete determination" of other concepts. He certainly does not mean to say that the concept of God we actually possess is one on which we have a firm grasp, or one whose content is transparent to us. On the contrary, he repeatedly asserts that we have only the poorest concept of supreme reality, and sometimes even insists that we have "no concept at all" of God.[79]

Such remarks as this last one, however, need to be understood in the context of Kant's theory of concepts. What Kant means by them is that since our concept of God is an idea of reason, no sensible content corresponding to it can ever be

78. *Gesammelte Schriften*, 28, 2, 2, p. 997; *Lectures on Philosophical Theology*, p. 25.
79. *Gesammelte Schriften*, 28, 2, 2, p. 996; *Lectures on Philosophical Theology*, p. 24.

given. This concept is thus an "empty" or "problematic" one, a concept incapable of serving as a vehicle of (empirical) knowledge. It is a concept through which an object may be *thought* but not *known*. In this, of course, the concept of God is no different from other ideas of reason, such as that of a free will, or the thinking self, or indeed from the concept of any object regarded as a mere noumenon, independently of its mode of givenness in our sensible intuition.

There are special difficulties, however, associated with the concept of God, or rather with the demands commonly made on it by rational theology. Philosophers do not usually trouble themselves about the "attributes" of a free will, for instance, beyond those directly required for its character as free. In the case of a supremely real being, however, philosophical theologians are often not content unless they can be quite specific about the properties which are involved in the possession of supreme reality. Is the most real being simple, or is it composed of parts? Can it undergo change? How is it related to space, time, and things different from it (if indeed there really are such)? Is the supreme being conscious or unconscious? Does it have knowledge or will? If so, what and how does it know and desire? In the *Lectures on Philosophical Theology* Kant asks all these traditional questions and tries to answer them. The *Lectures*, in fact, are our only real source for Kant's views on many of these matters, and it is perhaps surprising to see how sympathetic he is with the traditions of scholastic and rationalist theology as represented in Baumgarten's text.

On the basis of a Kantian epistemology, it might look as if there is very little we can be entitled to say about the divine attributes. For according to critical doctrines, all the properties of which we can form any determinate conception are phenomenal realities, which are necessarily limited in their degree. We have no acquaintance with any of the *realitates noumena* which lie behind these appearances; and consequently no determinate conception of the properties which belong to an *ens realissimum*.

These strictures, however, do not really apply to some predicates, such as those based on the categories, or on the "pure

derivative concepts," such as duration and change.[80] For although such concepts are "empty" ones in their application
to noumena, they are nevertheless available to us a priori as
formal elements of our concept of a thing or object in general.
Kant gives the name "ontological predicates" to these "a priori
realities" which belong to God in virtue of the fact that they
"refer to the universal attributes of a thing in general."[81] Kant's
list of ontological predicates, however, does not correspond
strictly to this account. For it includes not only substance, possibility, and presence, which arguably do belong to "the universal attributes of a thing in general," but also simplicity, im-
mutability, eternity, and extramundaneity, which clearly do not.
Yet these predicates, like those belonging indifferently to every
object, are constituted entirely of concepts which Kant classifies
as a priori ones. In them, these concepts are employed in ways
necessary to express the attributes of a noumenon and a supremely real being. The concepts of change and causal power,
for instance, are for Kant pure concepts or "predicables of pure
understanding" derived from the categories. To a thing whose
existence is not temporal, the concept of change is necessarily
inapplicable. And since time is merely a form of sensibility, applicable solely to phenomena, a purely noumenal being, such as
an *ens realissimum*, is necessarily changeless or immutable.[82]
Similarly, if we take every causal power to be essentially a reality or positive property, it follows that a supremely real being
must possess all such powers, and hence that it is omnipotent.
Not all the ontological predicates Kant ascribes to God apply
so straightforwardly, however. Kant's argument that the *ens
realissimum* is an *ens extramundanum*, for instance, relies on the
testimony of each person's self-consciousness to establish that
the thinking self is a finite substance, and consequently a part
of a world diverse from the infinite being.[83] But this testi-

80. *Critique of Pure Reason*, A 81f/B 107f.
81. *Gesammelte Schriften*, 28, 2, 2, p. 1020; *Lectures on Philosophical Theology*,
p. 51.
82. *Gesammelte Schriften*, 28, 2, 2, p. 1038; *Lectures on Philosophical Theology*,
p. 71.
83. *Gesammelte Schriften*, 28, 2, 2, p. 1041; *Lectures on Philosophical Theology*,
p. 74.

mony seems, on strict Kantian principles, not to be available. For it is argued in the Paralogisms that our mere self-consciousness entitles us to draw no conclusions at all about the nature of "the I or he or it" which is the transcendental subject of our thoughts.[84] Yet if there are problems regarding particular ontological predicates, it still remains true generally that there is nothing in principle which stands in the way of our using categories or other pure concepts to frame a notion of the supremely real being.

Kant gives the name "ontotheology" or "transcendental theology" to any theology which limits itself to an inventory of God's ontological predicates. And he regards such a theology as useful from a moral and religious standpoint, in that it prevents us from adopting an "anthropomorphic" conception of God, one drawn from empirical principles. Kant seems to have thought that theology, along with morality, becomes corrupted when it bases itself on empirical principles, and that when men draw their God from nature and experience rather than from pure reason they are more likely to serve him by empty ceremonies than by rational and morally upright conduct. For most peoples, he declares, the concept of God drawn from experience has served mainly as "a terrifying picture of fantasy, and a superstitious object of ceremonial adoration and hypocritical high praise." Transcendental theology, according to Kant, helps to rescue us from this sort of corrupt religion by supplying us with a more sober and austere notion of the divine, based on pure concepts of the understanding.[85]

But this does not mean that for Kant we can be satisfied, from a moral and religious standpoint, with transcendental theology all by itself. For its concept of God is "deistic"; it is merely the concept of a supremely real ground or cause of the world. Moral faith, in Kant's view, requires "theism," the belief in a "living God," a being endowed with knowledge and free volition, who governs the world wisely according to moral laws. For this reason, it is necessary to ascribe to God not only ontological predi-

84. *Critique of Pure Reason*, A 346/B 404.
85. *Gesammelte Schriften*, 28, 2, 2, p. 1046; *Lectures on Philosophical Theology*, p. 80.

cates drawn from pure understanding, but also "cosmological" or "psychological" predicates drawn from our empirical acquaintance with the human self or soul as a part of nature. Transcendental theology, says Kant, is an indispensable "propaedeutic" to a fuller theology, but remains "idle and useless" from a moral-religious point of view unless supplemented by it.[86]

In the *Beweisgrund* essay Kant held that it can be demonstrated that understanding and volition belong to the supreme reality which belongs to the ground of all possibility.[87] Essentially the same argument is given in the *Lectures* when Kant justified our ascription of psychological predicates to God on the ground that "in the whole of our experience we find nothing which has more reality than our own soul."[88] Later, however, he is more cautious on this point. He notes that we can never determine with certainty whether "the reality of a faculty of knowledge does not cancel any of the other realities when put together with them." Nevertheless he argues that "an *ens originarium* containing within itself the ground of the possibility of all things must have a faculty of knowledge because it is the original source of beings which do have this faculty (for example, men). For how could something be derived from a being unless this original being itself had it?" Kant admits, however, that we cannot refute "with apodictic certainty" the deist's claim that "there could be another kind of reality in the original source of things which might give rise to the faculty of knowledge inhering in human beings." The final, but somewhat tentative, conclusion is that we are entitled to ascribe a faculty of knowledge to God, so long as we admit that it is "wholly different" from the human faculty.[89]

But with this conclusion, the difficulties we raised earlier return in full force. For now Kant really does expect us to apply to God certain *realitates noumena* lying at the ground of phenomenal realities with which we are acquainted by experience. How,

86. *Gesammelte Schriften*, 28, 2, 2, p. 1002; *Lectures on Philosophical Theology*, p. 30.

87. *Gesammelte Schriften*, 2:87f.

88. *Gesammelte Schriften*, 28, 2, 2, p. 1020; *Lectures on Philosophical Theology*, p. 51.

89. *Gesammelte Schriften*, 28, 2, 2, p. 1050; *Lectures on Philosophical Theology*, p. 84.

on Kantian principles, can it be possible for us to form the concepts of such properties?

This problem, despite its Kantian setting, is a traditional one for rational theology. For it is customary to regard the divine attributes as utterly transcending the ordinary concepts which are applicable to created things. And Kant's solution to the problem is equally traditional. He holds that predicates drawn from phenomena can be applied to God if certain restrictions and qualifications are duly observed. First, he says, we must proceed by the *via negationis* to separate all limitations from the predicates we select. In the case of many of the properties of sensible things, this cannot be done without "canceling the concept" altogether; and properties of this kind cannot be predicated of God at all.[90] To the properties of extension, shape, and locomotion, for example, belong the limitations inherent in spatial existence. If we attempt to remove these negative qualities, the result is "nonspatial extension" and similar contradictory concepts. By contrast, Kant holds, we get no such contradictory results in the case of certain other properties, such as knowledge, volition, and moral goodness. These properties, then, may be applied to God. But, Kant insists, they must be applied by the *via eminentiae*. "For instance, not merely power, but *infinite* power must be ascribed to God, and not merely an understanding, but an *infinite* understanding."[91] The properties of finite things must be revised or modified to accord with the nature of an infinitely real being if we are to be able to ascribe them to God. Once again, if a property cannot survive this modification, it cannot be literally ascribed to God at all.

Most of Kant's detailed discussion of God's particular attributes in the *Lectures* concerns the ways in which the concepts applicable to finite things must be modified in order to "separate all sensible limitations" from them. Every faculty of knowledge, for example, requires according to Kant a faculty of intuition,

90. *Gesammelte Schriften*, 28, 2, 2, p. 1021; *Lectures on Philosophical Theology*, p. 52.

91. *Gesammelte Schriften*, 28, 2, 2, p. 1022; *Lectures on Philosophical Theology*, p. 53.

through which objects of knowledge can be immediately "given" to the knower. In human beings, this faculty is sensible—that is, passive, a receptivity to the effects objects have on us. The human understanding, which is a spontaneous or active faculty, is limited in its function to ordering the sensibly given data of knowledge according to discursive concepts, or universals. But only a limited being can be passive with respect to things outside itself. The concept of supreme reality precludes a faculty of knowledge which is in any part sensible. God's intuition, his immediate cognitive contact with objects, must therefore be spontaneous or active, a function of his understanding. Likewise, knowledge by means of universal concepts pertains only to finite beings, whose immediate acquaintance with objects provides them with information only in the form of certain general marks or characteristics of those objects. My sensible acquaintance with a certain body, for instance, provides me with knowledge of its color (white), its shape (spherical), and other such qualities. Each of them is a universal which may be shared by indefinitely many other bodies as well as by the one I am presently perceiving. Further investigation of the properties of the body, especially when aided by scientific theories, may reveal a great many other qualities. But this accumulation of information always consists in the further "determination" of the body by predicates expressing universal concepts. God's intuitive understanding, however, immediately grasps the thoroughly determined individual concept, the individual complete with all its properties in their particularity. It has no need for the discursive activity of thought, or the universal concepts framed by this activity.[92]

Because God's relation to the objects of his knowledge is wholly active rather than receptive, it follows that God's knowledge is entirely a priori.[93] It follows too that God's knowledge of things outside him is derived from his own self-knowledge:

92. *Gesammelte Schriften*, 28, 2, 2, p. 1053; *Lectures on Philosophical Theology*, p. 86.
93. *Gesammelte Schriften*, 28, 2, 2, p. 1051; *Lectures on Philosophical Theology*, p. 85.

his knowledge of possibles derives from knowledge of his own being as the *ens originarium*, the ground of all possibility.[94] And his knowledge of what is actual derives from his knowledge of his own free will in creating it exactly as he represents it to himself. God's knowledge, then, causes the truth of what it knows, and does this by means of its own representation of the objects of this knowledge. Since, however, volition is on the Kantian definition "the faculty of causing objects by means of their representations," it follows that God's understanding is identical with his will.[95]

But there is no space here to undertake a thorough discussion of Kant's treatment of the divine understanding and will, and the relations between them. The purpose of the above remarks is only to illustrate the manner in which Kant carries out the task of "separating the limitations" from the properties of creatures before applying them to the highest being. The important thing to recognize is that any such account of the divine attributes for Kant is fundamentally a way of telling us how the properties of God must be *unlike* those of creatures. They give us no positive information about the constitution of the divine attributes. Even the *via eminentiae*, says Kant, brings us no closer to any knowledge of how the divine attributes are constituted "in themselves." Such pure realities "cannot in general be comprehended by us at all." Thus none of the realities abstracted by us from the world of sense can be ascribed to God directly or univocally. The terms we use to signify the divine attributes must be applied to God with a purely *analogical* significance.[96]

Many Thomists, using a terminology somewhat at odds with that of Aquinas himself, draw a distinction between two sorts of analogical predication: the *analogy of attribution* and the *analogy of proportion*.[97] According to the former, mundane properties are

94. *Gesammelte Schriften*, 28, 2, 2, p. 1053; *Lectures on Philosophical Theology*, p. 89.

95. *Gesammelte Schriften*, 28, 2, 2, p. 1061; *Lectures on Philosophical Theology*, p. 97. Cf. *Gesammelte Schriften*, 5:9n, and *Critique of Practical Reason*, trans. L. W. Beck (Indianapolis, 1956), p. 9n.

96. *Gesammelte Schriften*, 28, 2, 2, p. 1023; *Lectures on Philosophical Theology*, p. 54.

97. Aquinas distinguishes between *analogia secundum convenientiam propor-*

predicated of God insofar as they bear a real (though of course imperfect) resemblance to the divine attributes. Thus we can attribute wisdom to God, employing a concept derived from our acquaintance with human wisdom, because the latter is an imperfect version of one of God's actual properties. In this analogy human wisdom is called the "prime analogate" because it is from it that we draw the concept which we apply to God, recognizing that the property we ascribe to him thereby is only imperfectly signified by the analogue which we use to get at it.

On the other hand, when we apply a predicate to God according to an analogy of proportion, we do not base our predication directly on any supposed similarity between the creaturely property from which the concept is drawn and the divine attribute we mean to designate. Instead, we base it on the fact that a certain relation in which God stands to his creatures is similar to a relation which some creature is known to stand to some other. And we predicate of God the properties appropriate to the corresponding relation, without implying that the designated properties of God are themselves similar to the creaturely ones in question. The standard illustration of this in St. Thomas is the application of the term "healthy" to the body, to medicine, and to urine.[98] Here the "prime analogate" is the health of the body, and the other two predications are based on it. We do not call medicine or urine "healthy" because they have in them any property resembling the health of the body. Instead, we call medicine "healthy" because it bears the relation "cause of" to the body's health; and we call urine "healthy" because it bears the relation "sign of" to this same property of the body. In practice, the relation employed in the theological use of this sort of analogy is nearly always that of cause and effect. God is, for instance, the cause of the wisdom in his creatures. And when, using the analogy of proportion, we ascribe wisdom to God, we

---

tionis and *analogia secundum convenientiam proportionalitatis*. See F. C. Copleston, *A History of Philosophy* (Garden City, N.Y., 1962), vol. 2, pt. 2, pp. 75f. Aquinas' "analogy according to resemblance of proportion" is usually called "analogy of attribution" and his "analogy according to resemblance of proportionality" is called "analogy of proportion."

98. *Summa Theologiae*, Ia Q. 13, a. 5, Resp.

do not ascribe to God any property resembling creaturely wisdom; we say only that God stands to this wisdom in the same relation as mundane causes stand to their effects.

Thomists usually hold that we can apply predicates analogically to God in either of these ways, or in both simultaneously. Kant, however, is emphatic in rejecting the analogy of attribution altogether and relying solely on the analogy of proportion. "Analogy," he says, "does not consist in an imperfect similarity of things to one another, as it is commonly taken." Instead, declares Kant, we must "assume analogy to be the perfect similarity of relations (not of things, but of relations) or, in short, what the mathematicians understand as proportion." [99] God's relationship to creatures, however, can only be conceived of in terms of pure categories, or ontological predicates. For otherwise, the relation itself would have to be predicated by analogy of proportion, and we would seem to have altogether lost our grip on the predicates we want to apply to God. [100] Fortunately, the relation of cause and effect (or ground and consequence) belongs to the categories of relation. And it seems to be the only relation Kant finds suitable for the purpose of analogical predication. [101]

99. *Gesammelte Schriften*, 28, 2, 2, p. 1023; *Lectures on Philosophical Theology*, p. 54.

100. *Gesammelte Schriften*, 4:357n; cf. *Prolegomena to Any Future Metaphysics*, ed. L. W. Beck (Indianapolis, 1950), p. 106n. Unlike Kant, most Thomists (including St. Thomas himself) hold that *every* proposition about God involves analogical predication. Presumably this is because the Thomists' empiricism is more thoroughgoing than Kant's; for St. Thomas holds that all our concepts are derived through the senses. Anyone who holds the Thomistic view on this point, however, seems to be threatened with incoherence if, like Kant, he treats the analogy of proportion as the exclusive (or even the fundamental) kind of analogical predication. Copleston thus seems to me correct when he criticizes certain Thomists who, while holding the view that all predications of God are analogical, also insist that the analogy of proportion is the fundamental kind of analogy: "I do not see how we could know that God has any perfection save by way of the analogy of attribution. All analogical predication rests on the real relation and likeness of creatures to God, and it seems to me that the analogy of proportionality presupposes analogy of proportion or attribution and that the latter is the more fundamental of the two kinds of analogy" (*History of Philosophy*, vol. 2, pt. 2, p. 76).

101. *Gesammelte Schriften*, 4:363n; cf. *Prolegomena*, p. 108n. In the *Lectures* Kant takes up analogy at just the point where Eberhard's text discusses the *via causalitatis* (pretty evidently just another name for the analogy of proportion).

But just how is Kant's analogical predication supposed to work? The matter is unfortunately not made at all clear. Kant apparently conceives of God's analogical predicates as drawn from the specific relation of finite causes to their effects:

If I say we are required to regard the world *as if* it were the work of a highest understanding and will, then I really say nothing more than that a watch, a ship, a regiment, bears the same relation to the artisan, the builder, the commander as the sensible world (or everything which goes to make up the foundation of this sum of appearances) bears to the unknown thing which I thus do not know as it is in itself but only as it is for me, that is, in regard to the world of which I am a part.[102]

Following this suggestion, any analogical predication would have two requirements: (1) the specification of a pair of causally related things in the phenomenal world (such as the benevolence of one man and the resultant happiness of another); and (2) the specification of something in the world (such as human happiness generally) which can be regarded as standing in a relation to God similar to the relation of the effect to the cause in the pair cited. One would then predicate of God the property (in this case, benevolence) in virtue of which the worldly cause specified in (1) produces its effect. But of course one would do this with respect to the effect of God's causality specified in (2). (In the passage just quoted, the pairs *watch: artisan*, *ship: builder* and so on would seem to specify the causal relation, and the sensible world—or its order and coherence—the divine effect. The point of the analogy seems to be to ascribe intelligence and planning, or understanding and volition, to God, with respect to his causing the world's order.)

This sort of account, however, invites a number of thorny questions. How are we to decide which causal pairs are appropriate to the analogical representation of God's attributes? And

---

Of the three categories of relation (substance/accident, cause/effect, causal reciprocity) only the second admits of an (orthodox) application to the relation between God and creatures. To apply the substance/accident relation in this context is to fall into Spinozism, which both Kant and his textbooks vehemently reject. Causal reciprocity between God and his creatures is ruled out because God's supreme perfection renders him "impassible." *Gesammelte Schriften*, 28, 2, 2, p. 1043; *Lectures on Philosophical Theology*, p. 76.

102. *Gesammelte Schriften*, 4:357; cf. *Prolegomena*, p. 106.

how do we know which aspects of the sensible world we are justified in regarding as analogous to the effect in each pair? Further, not everything analogically predicated of God is obviously causal in the way this account requires. No doubt benevolence and intelligent design have causal implications of the right kind. But we also ascribe purely contemplative knowledge to God, even though its human analogue is not (or at least not essentially) a cause of anything.

Sometimes, however, Kant seems to be suggesting that analogical predication has no such strict requirements as those which give rise to these questions. In some passages he seems to be saying instead that when we ascribe an analogical predicate to God, what we are really saying is only that God is the cause of the creaturely property designated by that predicate, without our being able to specify any more precisely than this what sort of causal relation is involved. Perhaps this is what he means when he says: "For just as in the world one thing is regarded as the cause of another thing when it contains the ground for that thing, so in the same way we regard the whole world as a consequence of its ground in God, and argue from the analogy." [103] Kant does say too that "the concept of relation in this case is a mere category, that is, the concept of cause, which has nothing to do with sensibility." [104] This may mean merely that every analogical predication rests on a nonanalogical one, namely, the ontological predicate of causality. But it may also mean that, contrary to the apparent implications of the passage we looked at earlier, nothing belonging to any particular causal relations in the world of sense (e.g., *watch: artisan*) can be included in the content of the analogical predicate. On this account, we would predicate wisdom of God simply because he is taken to be the cause of the wisdom in his creatures. And we could just as easily predicate contemplative knowledge (or other noncausal properties) of him, since he is equally the cause of those properties in the things that have them.

This use of analogy, however, is also open to question. Ac-

103. *Gesammelte Schriften*, 28, 2, 2, p. 1023; *Lectures on Philosophical Theology*, p. 54.

104. *Gesammelte Schriften*, 4:357n; cf. *Prolegomena*, p. 106n.

cording to F. C. Copleston, "we do not predicate wisdom of God merely because God is the cause of all wise things, for in that case we might just as well call God a stone, as being the cause of all stones."[105] In reply to this, of course, Kant would insist that there are a great many mundane predicates which we cannot apply to God at all, even if God is the cause of the properties they signify, on account of the strictures noted above in connection with the *via eminentiae*. For one provision of the *via eminentiae* is that no predicate can be applied to God unless it can without contradiction be conceived of as admitting of a supreme or infinite degree. "Wisdom," Kant would argue, is a predicate which will pass this test, while "stone" is not. Nevertheless, Kant's view still falls prey to Copleston's objection. For it seems to be right to say that we do not predicate wisdom (or anything else) of God merely because God causes wisdom in creatures, but also because we take God himself to have this same property (or some property of which human wisdom is an imperfect copy). The whole point of the *via eminentiae* would appear to be that in our selection of predicates for God, we want to be sure to choose only those such that an infinitely perfect being might actually have them, or have some supremely perfect version of them. The provision that divine attributes must be designated by predicates admitting of a supreme degree would have no clear point unless to guarantee that no absurdity will result from our supposing that God actually has an attribute somehow resembling the finite creaturely one from which we draw its concept. The provision would hardly be necessary if all we meant in saying "God is F" is that God is the cause of the F-ness in finite things. For God is equally the cause of properties that admit of a supreme degree and of properties that do not; and we would honor his causal power as much by the mention of the one sort of creaturely property as by mention of the other.

Even Kant's most extended discussions of analogical predication, in the *Lectures* and the *Prolegomena*, are too brief for us to have any very clear idea of what he took the doctrine of analogy to be. One suspects that in these comparatively popular works,

---

105. *History of Philosophy*, vol. 2, pt. 2, p. 75.

Kant merely took over the theory of analogy from tradition, without working out its details with any great care. One thing, however, is clear: Kant intends the main thrust of the theory to be in the direction of a rather extreme agnosticism regarding the nature of the divine attributes. Kant's rejection of the analogy of attribution implies that for him when we predicate benevolence of God, or wisdom, or understanding, we do not have any right to claim that there is in God any property actually resembling the human qualities which go by those names. Rather, we say at most that there is in God something (we know not what) which causes human happiness or cosmic order, just as the happiness of a human being or the mechanical structure of a watch are caused by human charity or art. As Kant puts it: "The expression suited to our feeble concepts is that we think of the world *as if* its existence and inner determination were derived from a highest reason, through which . . . we come to know the constitution belonging to the world, but without presuming to determine its cause as it is in itself." [106]

At this point, the impact of Kant's moral theology is evident. Kant was convinced that an upright moral disposition rationally required belief in a moral world, purposively ordered by a supremely wise and morally perfect being, very much along the lines of the God of traditional theistic religions. At the same time, his moral convictions as a partisan of the Enlightenment made him highly skeptical of popular religions. He was persuaded that the superstition, fanaticism, hypocrisy, and slavish devotion he condemned in them was at least in good part a result of their defective concept of God, a concept which was corrupted because, unlike the moral law which should have been its rational standard, it was derived from empirical sources. The remedy for popular religion, from this point of view, was a stricter adherence to a wholly a priori theology. In view of Kant's critical strictures on the human ability even to conceive of transcendent or wholly nonsensuous objects, this necessitated a theology of an especially dry and austere kind, in which everything involving "mere human representations" had been

106. *Gesammelte Schriften*, 4:359; cf. *Prolegomena*, p. 108.

carefully removed, and as little as possible had been conceded to the overheated imagination of the popular cults.

It may seem paradoxical that, on the one hand, Kant should have so strenuously insisted on a concept of God so precisely determined from the moral and metaphysical view as an onto-logically perfect intelligent volitional agent possessed of su-preme holiness, benevolence, and justice; while on the other hand he was so anxious to render this concept as empty, vague, and indefinite as possible by placing it beyond the power of our faculties to comprehend. The paradox, however, is hardly unique to Kant, and seems to belong in one form or other to the whole Western tradition of orthodox rational theology, which usually combined its detailed inventory of divine attributes with an extreme degree of agnosticism about the real nature of what was being inventoried. Here again, if Kant's rational theology is faced with insuperable difficulties, it is not likely that other adherents of the tradition will fare much better.

2. The Three Theistic Proofs

The best known part of Kant's rational theology is its negative part: the famous refutations of the received arguments for God's existence. Above all, it was this side of Kant which gave the critical philosophy the "world destroying" impact, as Heine dramatically put it, on its own and the succeeding century. But Kant's aim here as elsewhere was to be as systematic and thorough as possible. His critique of speculative theism was not simply a series of attacks on the particular theistic proofs which had been offered by earlier philosophers. Its purpose was to show not only that no such proofs had in fact succeeded, but also that no speculative proofs of any kind for God's existence have any prospect of succeeding.

According to Kant, our concept of God, like the other ideas of reason, is necessarily an "empty" or "problematic" one, a concept *ohne Sinn und Bedeutung*, devoid of sensible content and possible empirical reference. When Kant describes this concept as "problematic" he means to imply that it sets us a problem without a solution, because we can never expect to obtain knowledge of the existence or the properties of any object corresponding to it. At times it seems that Kant means to draw this skeptical conclusion simply from the fact that the ideas of reason are "empty" and necessarily devoid of sensible content. Ideas of reason, he says, are concepts through which objects may be *thought*, but not *known*, as if it followed merely from the fact that no sensible referents for such concepts can be given in our experience that we can never establish the existence or non-existence of the corresponding objects, or determine the properties belonging to them.[1]

If Kant does mean to argue in this fashion, however, he never tells us explicitly what his argument is. Perhaps his view is that since all the synthetic principles we might use to obtain such knowledge are either derived from experience or recognized as conditions of its possibility, none of them can be trusted in arguments concerned with objects transcending the empirical world. Kant could certainly have found this line of thinking expressed in the writings of Hume. But he could just as surely have found it disputed by a philosopher such as St. Thomas Aquinas, who found nothing wrong with reasoning from empirically derived principles about motion, causality, and perfection to conclusions about a first being who can never be an object of sense experience, or even of univocal description in concepts derived from the senses. Moreover, it is not in the least obvious that Aquinas is mistaken on this point. For why should we be hesitant to draw conclusions which follow naturally from the most certain and comprehensive principles we have, whatever their source?

Theistic arguments, even the most abstract and a priori of them, cannot be dismissed simply by appealing in some vague way to an empiricist epistemology. It is to Kant's credit that he does not take this route when he attempts to establish the impossibility of any theoretical demonstration of God's existence. Instead, he proceeds by dividing all possible theistic proofs into kinds, and arguing in each case that no successful proof of that kind can be given.

Kant's Strategy

Kant says that there are fundamentally three possible proofs for the existence of an *ens realissimum*; (1) the *ontological*, which

1. *Critique of Pure Reason*, B xxviii, A 336/B 393, A 348f, A 609/B 637, A 646/B 619f.

"abstracts from all experience and argues wholly a priori from mere concepts"; (2) the *cosmological*, which "is grounded empirically only on an indeterminate experience, i.e., on some existence or other"; and (3) the *physicotheological*, which "begins from determinate experience and the constitution of our particular sensible world."[2] For Kant's aim in Sections 3 through 6 of the Ideal of Pure Reason is to show that none of these proofs can succeed. His strategy is first to undermine the ontological proof and then to argue that both the other proofs tacitly presuppose it, so that its failure, by a kind of domino effect, guarantees the failure of all possible speculative proofs for the existence of a supreme being.

To this end, Kant distinguishes in both the cosmological and physicotheological arguments two steps or stages: the first stage argues from some experience to the existence of a being of a certain description, and the second stage argues that any being of that description must be an *ens realissimum*. More specifically, the cosmological argument (in Kant's Wolffian version of it) begins with the empirical fact that some contingent thing (myself, or a world in general) exists. It proceeds to argue that since what is contingent must have a cause, a ground, or sufficient reason for its being rather than not being, and since an infinite regress of contingent causes or grounds is untenable, there must exist a necessary being to serve as the first cause or sufficient ground of everything contingent.[3] This completes the first stage of the cosmological argument. The second stage argues that the necessary being demonstrated in the first stage has to be an *ens realissimum*. In parallel fashion, the physicotheological argument begins with the order, harmony, and beauty of the natural world, and concludes that they can be explained only by supposing there to be an intelligence from whose wisdom, power, and free volition such purposes proceed. This constitutes the first stage of the argument. The second stage has the task of showing this intelligence to be an *ens realissimum*.

2. *Critique of Pure Reason*, A 590/B 619f.
3. Cf. Wolff, *Metaphysik* (Halle, 1751), vol. 1, §928, pp. 574f. Cf. *Theologia Naturalis* (Frankfurt and Leipzig, 1730) 1, §69, p. 55.

Curiously enough, Kant provides no detailed criticism of the first stage of either of these two proofs and seems to grant, at least for the sake of argument, both the inference from some contingent existence to a necessary being and the inference from the orderliness found in nature to a designing intelligence. These concessions, however, can be explained by Kant's overall strategy. It is only the second stage of each proof, in his view, which presupposes the ontological proof. The domino effect in which Kant is interested provides no refutation of the arguments for a necessary being or an intelligent designer of the natural order, but applies only to reason's attempt to identify these beings with an *ens realissimum*.

This does not mean that Kant really accepts the first stage of either argument. On the inference from contingent to necessary existence, he enumerates four objections drawn from doctrines already expounded in the *Critique*. None of these objections, however, is clearly decisive, and Kant himself appears to admit that they are too tersely expressed to amount to a definitive refutation.[4] Doubts are also expressed about the analogical reasoning involved in the first stage of the design argument, and Kant suggests that it "perhaps could not withstand the sharpest transcendental critique." Once again, however, his objections are no more than hinted at.[5]

4. "A little earlier I said that in this cosmological argument there lies hidden a whole nest of dialectical presumptions, which a transcendental critique can easily discover and destroy. Now I shall merely specify them, and leave it to the reader, who is already used to this, to inquire further into these deceptive principles and to do away with them" (*Critique of Pure Reason*, A 609/B 637). Kant then proceeds to list four such "deceptive principles" or "dialectical presumptions": (1) the employment of the principle that everything contingent has a cause. "This principle," Kant asserts, "is applicable only in the sensible world; outside that world it has no significance whatever" (cf. A 216ff/B 263ff). (2) "The inference to a first cause from the impossibility of an infinite series of causes." This inference, in Kant's view, is not justified "even in the world of experience" (cf. A 308/B 364; A 448ff/B 476ff). (3) "The unjustified self-satisfaction of reason with regard to the completion of this series" (cf. A 612ff/B 640); and (4) the "confusion" of logical with real possibility with respect to the concept of an *ens realissimum* (cf. *Gesammelte Schriften*, 28, 2, 2, pp. 1023ff; *Lectures on Philosophical Theology*, trans. Allen W. Wood and Gertrude M. Clark (Ithaca, N.Y., 1978), p. 54ff.

5. Kant suggests that in the physicotheological proof we may "do violence to

Kant's strategy was formulated with the aim of systematizing his critique of speculative theology as much as possible. But however well it may succeed on this score, it carries with it a couple of serious disadvantages. First, the power of Kant's critique of the cosmological and physicotheological proof is radically dependent on his criticism of the ontological proof. If (as I mean to argue) this criticism should prove to be less than conclusive, then Kant really provides no effective criticism at all of the other two proofs. No doubt Kant was persuaded that the ontological proof is the least persuasive of the three, and the proof whose weaknesses could be most easily shown up. But it just might be that the ontological proof is less vulnerable than the other two in certain ways, and that even if they do depend on it, their shortcomings could be more easily displayed by independent criticisms. A second disadvantage of Kant's strategy is even more serious. By leaving virtually unchallenged the arguments for a necessary being and an intelligent designer of nature, Kant is in effect conceding some very controversial points to the speculative theist. Kant himself always thought that a theology which fell short of establishing the supreme ontological perfection of the divine being would have to be judged a complete failure. The positive side of his own rational theology, both in its metaphysical and its moral aspects, provided him, as we have seen above, with powerful reasons for thinking this. Nevertheless, it is entirely possible that speculative theologians might disagree with him, and it is hard to deny that if we could demonstrate that there is a necessarily existent cause of the world and intelligent author of its order, this result would have considerable philosophical interest, even if it could not be shown that this being is an *ens realissimum*. On both counts, the scope of Kant's "world destroying" criticism of the traditional theistic proofs is sharply limited by his strategy of

nature, requiring it to behave not in accordance with its own ends, but to fit with ours (by similarity with houses, ships, watches, and so on)"; he also finds questionable the inference that "the inner possibility of a freely operating nature (which first makes art, and perhaps even reason itself, possible) is derived from yet another, though superhuman, art" (*Critique of Pure Reason*, A 626/B 654).

focusing his attacks on the ontological argument as the "only possible ground of proof" for God's existence.

The Ontological Proof

Descartes' Most Baffling Argument

In his Second Reply to Objections, Descartes sets forth his Fifth Meditation proof for God's existence in the following syllogism:

Major Premise
> Whatever we clearly understand to pertain to the nature of anything can with truth be affirmed of that thing.

Minor Premise
> But it pertains to the nature of God that he exists.

Conclusion
> Therefore, it can with truth be affirmed of God that he exists.[6]

The major premise of this syllogism is based on Descartes' criterion for certainty, that a proposition is known by us with perfect certainty when we "intuit" or "clearly and distinctly apprehend" its truth.[7] It is also based on his view that the mind has innately present to it the ideas of what he calls "pure and simple essences" or "true and immutable natures."[8] These the intellect is capable of apprehending clearly and distinctly by a direct intuition, and they furnish it a priori with a stock of certain knowledge. Probably the best examples of such natures are furnished by mathematics. By inspecting the nature of a tri-

---

6. René Descartes, *Oeuvres*, ed. C. Adam and P. Tannery (Paris, 1904), 7:150; *Philosophical Works*, ed. Haldane and Ross (New York, 1955), 2:45; cf. *Oeuvres*, 7:166f; *Philosophical Works*, 2:57.

7. *Oeuvres*, 7:35; *Philosophical Works*, 1:157f; *Oeuvres*, 10:368, *Philosophical Works*, 1:7.

8. *Oeuvres*, 7:35; *Philosophical Works*, 1:157f; *Oeuvres*, 10:368, *Philosophical Works*, 1:15. The terms "intuition" and "pure and simple essence" are characteristic of Descartes' first essay on the subject, the *Rules for the Direction of the Mind*. The terms "clear and distinct apprehension" and "true and immutable nature" are characteristic of the *Meditations* and other later works.

angle, for example, the mind is able to perceive a priori and with complete certainty that it belongs necessarily to this figure to have its largest side opposite its largest angle, to have its interior angles equal to two right angles, and other such properties. Whatever attribute is clearly perceived to pertain to a true and immutable nature is thereby certainly known to belong to it.

But Descartes also holds that we have in our stock of ideas one which represents a being possessing every perfection. The minor premise of Descartes' syllogism is based on the intellectual inspection of the true and immutable nature of this supreme perfection, and the resultant perception that to exist belongs among the perfections pertaining to it. Descartes holds, indeed, that existence is a perfection belonging to *any* nature which does not involve a contradiction. He holds this because he believes, with Hume, that "to conceive a thing, and to conceive it as existing, are nothing different from one another."[9] If I form a mental image of a winged horse, for example, I picture it as it would look if it existed. If I conceive of a triangular body, I endow it in my thought with all the properties it would have if it were an actual thing. Of course, when I think of such things I do not necessarily believe that they exist, nor does it follow from the fact that I conceive them as existing that they really are actual things. This, according to Descartes, is because the sort of existence which belongs to them in thought is only "possible existence." That is, when I think of a triangular body as existing, I naturally think of it as having the sort of existence belonging to a thing whose being is contingent on the being and the causal efficacy of other things. If the triangular body I am thinking of were actually to exist, it would have to be produced by some cause external to itself, and its continued existence would be beholden to various causes and circumstances which sustain it. This contingency of existence is, on Descartes' view, built into the nature of all bodies and finite minds and pertains to our very thought of these things. Hence possible or contingent existence is one of the perfections which we clearly and distinctly apprehend when we conceive of any finite things.

9. Hume, *Treatise on Human Nature*, ed. Selby-Bigge (Oxford, 1967), p. 66.

The matter is different, however, when we turn our attention to the nature of a supremely perfect being. For we note that such a being, having every power, cannot be prevented from existing by any being, nor have its existence beholden to anything outside itself. It follows from God's omnipotence, according to Descartes, that "he can exist by his own power" and from this fact "we therefore conclude that he truly exists and has existed from eternity; for we know by the light of nature that what can exist by its own power always exists." [10] To the true and immutable nature of God, therefore, there pertains a higher and more perfect kind of existence than that pertaining to the nature of finite things. Whereas it belongs to the latter to have merely possible or contingent existence, it belongs to the nature of God to have necessary existence:

> For I do not doubt that whoever attends diligently to this diversity between the idea of God and that of everything else will perceive that although these other things are understood as existing, it still does not follow from this that they exist, but only that they can exist, because we do not understand that their necessary being is conjoined with their properties; yet because we understand that actual existence is necessarily and always conjoined with the remaining attributes of God, it does indeed follow that God exists. [11]

The ontological argument as Kant considers it is largely divested of its Cartesian niceties. It seems to amount simply to the claim that God exists because the proposition that God exists is an analytic proposition. "The argument," says Kant, "is this: An *ens realissimum* is something which contains all realities in itself. But existence is also a reality. Hence the *ens realissimum* must necessarily exist. Thus if someone were to assert that God does not exist, he would be negating in the predicate something which is included in the subject, and this would be a contradiction." [12]

In Kant's terminology, as we noted above, a proposition is

10. *Oeuvres*, 7:119; *Philosophical Works*, 2:21.
11. *Oeuvres*, 7:116f; *Philosophical Works*, 2:20.
12. *Gesammelte Schriften*, 28, 2, 2, p. 1027; *Lectures on Philosophical Theology*, p. 58.

analytic when the predicate is included or "contained" in the concept of the subject. [13] Every concept for Kant is made up of certain "marks" or "characteristics," consisting in various realities or their negations. The concept of body, for example, contains the characteristics of spatial extension, impenetrability, and shape. Hence when we assert the proposition "All bodies are extended," we are predicating of the subject something which is already contained in its own concept. Hence our proposition is analytic, and its denial involves a contradiction. Such a proposition, according to Kant, may be known to be true a priori, because nothing but an inventory of the subject concept is required for this knowledge. Certain other determinations, however, (e.g. weight and color) fall outside the content of the concept of body. Hence the propositions "All bodies are heavy" and "This body is colored" are synthetic. If they are true, the predicate must "belong to" or "be connected with" the subject concept, without being "contained in" it. And our judgment that such propositions are true, a judgment which "synthesizes" or "puts together" the subject concept and the predicate falling outside it, requires for its justification something else besides this concept. In the case of empirical judgments, this "something else" is our experience of the object. In the case of a priori synthetic judgments, according to Kant, the only available justification is an appeal to the conditions of any possible experience.

The ontological argument, as Kant seems to understand it, begins with the concept of God, a supremely perfect being or *ens realissimum*, a concept containing in it absolutely every reality and nothing at all in the way of imperfection or negation. Consequently, every judgment of the form "God is F" is analytic, and hence true a priori, granted only that F be a predicate consisting entirely of realities and involving no negations. But according to the argument, "being" or "existence" is a predicate of this sort. For to say that a thing *exists* or *is* is surely to say something unqualifiedly positive about it. Consequently, the proposition "God exists" is analytic, and thus true a priori.

13. *Critique of Pure Reason*, A 610/B 638.

Existence and Predication

The main thrust of Kant's attack on this argument seems to be the claim that all existential propositions must be synthetic. This criticism is well known, but Kant's own expression of it involves some difficult terminology and an unfamiliar logical setting. The principal error in the ontological proof, he contends, is its confusion of a "logical" predicate with a "real" predicate or "determination": "Anything we like," he says, "may serve as a logical predicate. . . . But a determination is a predicate which adds to the concept of the subject and increases it. Hence it must not be contained in it."[14]

For Kant, as we have seen, to "determine" the concept of a thing is to add to our stock of information about the thing by predicating something of it in accordance with some rational procedure. Anything whatever may serve as a "logical predicate," or occupy the predicate position in a sentence. But not everything may serve as a "real predicate" or "determination," as a predicate which, when "added" to a concept in a subject-predicate proposition, "determines" it, or gives us some new information about what belongs to it. But, according to Kant, no new information of this kind is provided when we say that a thing is or exists. "Being," he says, "is obviously no real predicate, that is, it is not the concept of anything which could be added to the concept of a thing."[15]

The relevance of these claims to the ontological argument, however, may not be immediately evident. For the argument, especially as Kant represents it, never claims that the predicate "exists" "determines" our concept of God in the sense of giving us new information about him, or "adding" something to our concept which was not already contained in it. On the contrary, the whole point of the ontological proof is to argue that "exists" is not a predicate which needs to be "added to" the concept of God, because it is precisely the contention of the proof that the proposition "God exists" is analytically true. The proof begins

14. *Critique of Pure Reason*, A 599/B 626.
15. *Critique of Pure Reason*, A 599/B 626; *Gesammelte Schriften*, 28, 2, 2, p. 1027; *Lectures on Philosophical Theology*, p. 59.

with the concept of an *ens realissimum* which, as Kant himself concedes, is already thoroughly determined a priori by its own content; and it draws the necessary existence of God out of this concept as one of the realities contained in it.

Kant's way of putting his criticism, in fact, even makes it seem as though he is claiming just the opposite of what he wants to prove. For if existence is not something which can be *added to* the concept of a thing, the only alternative, given Kant's conception of the structure of a proposition, is that it be something which is *contained in* its concept. But in that case, it would follow that *every* existential proposition is analytic. This, of course, is just the opposite of the view for which Kant is supposed to be arguing. And it is, besides, a view which is so obviously false that not even a proponent of the ontological argument will have a moment's hesitation in rejecting it.[16]

Yet such an interpretation of Kant's words must be mistaken, however natural it may be. When Kant denies that "exists" can be "added to" the concept of a thing, he clearly does not mean to commit himself to the view that all existential propositions are analytic, nor does he mean to deny (what everyone admits without dispute) that sometimes when we say things of the form "X exists" we are providing some new information about X. Kant's point can be appreciated, I think, if we approach his remarks from a different direction. He is proceeding on the supposition that the content of any concept must be drawn from the same stock of realities and negations which are available to us in the further determination of concepts. The contents of a concept, on his view, provide us with certain identifying marks which enable us to pick out an object for further determination.

16. Jerome Shaffer notes the apparent inconsistency in Kant's views: "What is a 'real' predicate? Kant defines it as something 'which is added to the concept of the subject and enlarges it'. This is a most unfortunate definition for Kant to use, however, since it leads to a contradiction with another important doctrine of his, that existential propositions are always synthetic. Synthetic judgments are those which 'add to the concept of the subject a predicate which has not been in any wise thought in it,' and if existential judgments are always synthetic then 'exists' must be a predicate which adds to the concept of the subject, in short, a 'real' predicate as defined above" ("Existence, Predication and the Ontological Argument," in *The First Critique*, ed. Terence Penelhum and J. J. McIntosh [Belmont, Calif., 1969], p. 125).

The concept "body," for instance, identifies a given particular as an extended, impenetrable thing with some shape or other; and, using this concept, we can go on to say of this particular that it is colored, heavy, and so on. Any such identifying mark, however, in Kant's view, must be a property which might (in another context) serve to add to our stock of information about what belongs to a concept. Hence if the (logical) predicate "exists" cannot serve to determine the concept of which it is predicated, then there can be no concept in which it figures as a content or identifying mark. And if this is the case, then no proposition of the form "X exists" can be analytic.

According to Kant, "being" or "existence" is not a determination, or real predicate. Hence it cannot serve as an identifying mark which might go to make up the content of some concept. Rather, it is "merely the positing of a thing, or of certain determinations, as existing in themselves. When we say "God is" or "There is a God," we attach no new predicate to the concept of God, but only posit the subject in itself with all its predicates." Existence, therefore, is not a reality or perfection. "The actual," according to Kant, "contains no more than the merely possible. A hundred actual dollars do not contain the least bit more than a hundred possible dollars. . . . But there is more in my financial position in the case of a hundred actual dollars than in the case of the mere concept of them." [17]

Kant's criticism thus depends on drawing a distinction between two sorts of synthetic propositions: (1) Those which "determine" the subject concept or "add to" it, by predicating some reality (or negation) of it; and (2) those which "posit" the concept or the determinations thought in it. In the former case, the determinations or "real predicates" which are applied to a thing may (in another context) serve as the contents of a subject concept. And, considering now only those which are made up of realities, we know a priori that any and all of them must belong to the thoroughly determined concept of an *ens realissimum*. If "is" or "exists" were a real predicate of this kind, then it could

17. *Critique of Pure Reason*, A 598ff/B 626ff; cf. *Gesammelte Schriften*, 28, 2, 2, p. 1028; *Lectures on Philosophical Theology*, p. 59.

not be denied that the proposition "God exists" is analytic. But, Kant maintains, when we assert that something exists, we do not ascribe any reality to it; we do not determine its concept by anything which could (in another context) go to make up the identifying marks constituting the content of a subject concept. Since existence is not a reality, we are not required to think it in the concept of an *ens realissimum*, and hence need not conclude that the existence of such a being is asserted by an analytic proposition. When we assert that something exists, we do not "add to" the subject concept, but only "posit" this concept or the determinations contained in it.

More recent philosophers have spoken not of "positing" but of declaring a concept "instantiated" or asserting that it "applies to something." Their point, however, seems to be the same as Kant's, and Kant is rightly credited with the same criticism of the ontological proof. Like Kant, they maintain that asserting that a thing exists is entirely different from ascribing any property to it. And they also mean to conclude from this that existence cannot be legitimately included in the concept of a thing. It cannot be one of the identifying marks of a thing, or part of the meaning of the word or description that signifies it, that its concept is instantiated, or that this word or description succeeds in referring or applying to something. From this conclusion, however, it follows as a matter of logic that no propositions asserting existence can be analytic ones.

Like most partisans of this view, Kant regards its truth as something obvious, something "every rational person admits." [18] Yet it cannot have been so obvious to Descartes and other proponents of the ontological argument. For surely Descartes knew that to say "God exists" is to say that the concept of God is instantiated, that the word "God" or the description "most real being" succeeds in referring or applying to something. Hence he must have believed, contrary to the Kantian view, that the necessary instantiation of a concept could be included among its contents. What argument does Kant give him for abandoning this belief?

18. *Critique of Pure Reason*, A 598/B 626.

Kant's only real argument (the only one I can find at any rate) is presented in the following passage:

No matter which and how many predicates I think in a thing (and even if I think it as completely determined), I still do not add the least bit to it when I posit that this thing *is*. For otherwise it would not be just the same thing I thought in my concept which exists, and I could not say that it is precisely the object of my concept which exists. If I think in a thing every reality but one, the missing reality is not added when I say that this defective thing exists. On the contrary, it exists encumbered with precisely the same defect I thought in it, since otherwise what exists would be something other than what I thought.[19]

Kant's argument may, I think, be fairly paraphrased as follows: Let us give the name "almost perfect being" to any entity which has every perfection but one. And let us suppose that we have before us the concept of such a being, only we do not know *which* reality is the missing one in the case of that particular almost perfect being. Now Kant's contention is that we are led into absurdities if we assume that "existence" is the reality we are seeking. For suppose it is. In that case, if the almost perfect being we are thinking of existed, it would have the missing reality, and therefore would not be almost perfect, but wholly perfect. But this contradicts the assumption that we are thinking of an *almost* perfect being, and hence is absurd. Existence, therefore, cannot be the reality we are looking for. But no restrictions whatever were placed on the reality missing from our almost perfect being. Consequently, if existence cannot be the missing reality, this can only be because existence is not a reality at all. And this is what Kant desired to prove.

Like Jerome Shaffer, I find it astonishing that this argument has stood up for so long, and that so many philosophers who are otherwise clearheaded and critical have found it convincing. We can see at once that it *cannot* be correct if we run through it again, this time supposing "omnipotence" (or any other undisputed real predicate) to be the reality missing from our almost perfect being. In that case too we would have to admit that if the almost perfect being were omnipotent, it would have the

19. *Critique of Pure Reason*, A 600/B 628; cf. *Gesammelte Schriften*, 28, 2, 2, p. 1028; *Lectures on Philosophical Theology*, pp. 59f.

missing reality, and hence be wholly perfect, contrary to our original supposition. Thus if Kant's argument succeeded in showing that existence is not a real predicate, it would also succeed in showing that nothing could be one.[20]

It seems to me that the supposed absurdity, in both cases, results from an ambiguity in "almost perfect being" or "being having every reality but one." Such expressions can mean either: (1) a being which has all realities but one, and does not necessarily have this one reality; or (2) a being which has all realities but one, and necessarily lacks this one reality. If it means (1) there is no absurdity at all in supposing that it has the missing reality (be that reality existence, omnipotence, or what you will). At most there would be a verbal contradiction, as when a shepherd says that the lost sheep has been found. On the other hand, if "almost perfect being" means (2), then there is an absurdity all right, but this absurdity has nothing to do with what we suppose the missing reality to be. It comes instead from our speculating what would be the case if the almost perfect being had a reality which *ex hypothesi* it necessarily lacks. However we read the argument it does absolutely nothing to show that existence is not a reality, perfection, or real predicate, or that propositions of the form "*X* exists" cannot be analytic.[21]

20. Shaffer, "Existence, Predication and the Ontological Argument," p. 126.

21. Shaffer has another diagnosis of Kant's error at this point: "The difficulty here lies in an incomplete picture of predication. Kant seems to think that when I say that so-and-so is such-and-such, I must be doing one of two things: either I am extracting the concept of such-and-such from the concept of so-and-so (an analytic judgment) or else I am revising my concept of so-and-so by adding to it the concept of such-and-such (a synthetic judgment). . . . But to say that so-and-so is such-and-such is sometimes neither to analyze the concept of so-and-so nor to revise it, but, to put it roughly, to say something about the object conceived of" (ibid.). Of course, when a philosopher makes a mistake in argument, it is sometimes difficult to locate precisely what went wrong. But it is certainly *not* Kant's view in general that synthetic propositions "revise" the subject concept to contain henceforth the predicate as part of this concept. (See Lewis W. Beck, "Can Kant's Synthetic Judgments Be Made Analytic?" in *Kant*, ed. Robert Paul Wolff [Garden City, N.Y., 1967], pp. 13f). Kant does hold, of course, that when we apply a predicate to a subject, we do assert that predicate to "belong to" or be "connected with" that concept, as part of the completely determined whole experience of the object which the subject concept designates. But as we noted above, he draws a sharp distinction between a predicate's "belonging to" a concept (as in a true synthetic judgment) and its "being contained in" the subject concept (as in an analytic judgment).

Kant does succeed in setting forth a view about existence and predication which, if it is correct, does rid us once and for all of the concept of logically necessary existence, and with it the ontological argument. But he provides us with no good reasons for thinking his view to be the correct one. Kant's view has been, and still is, widely accepted and is even (owing to its adoption by Gottlob Frege and Bertrand Russell) incorporated into the standard systems of formal logic, via the existence quantifier. Yet no one as far as I can tell has ever presented a really persuasive argument for it.

Partisans of the Kantian view often cite G. E. Moore's "tame tigers" example as providing evidence in its favor.[22] According to Moore, the sentence "Tame tigers growl" is ambiguous between "All tame tigers growl," "Most tame tigers growl," and "Some tame tigers growl." But, he alleges, there is no such ambiguity in the sentence "Tame tigers exist": it must mean "Some tame tigers exist" or "There are tame tigers." Moore thinks that such sentences as "All tame tigers exist" and "Most tame tigers exist" have no meaning at all, or at least no clear one.[23] An even more significant difference, in Moore's view, between "exists" and real properties (such as "growl" and "scratch") is brought out by comparing the (internal) negations of the sentences "Some tame tigers growl" and "Some tame tigers exist." According to Moore, "Some tame tigers do not growl" has a perfectly clear meaning; "Some tame tigers do not exist," however, has no meaning at all, or at least not a clear one. Moore admits that we can "give" this sentence a meaning, by including fictional or imaginary tame tigers within our universe of discourse. But, he contends, if we do this, we have "changed the meaning of 'exist'" in the two sentences.[24] Presumably what he has in mind here is that "Some tame tigers exist" can be taken as equivalent to "There are tame tigers," but the (internal) negation of the former sentence cannot be taken to be equivalent to the negation of the latter.

22. G. E. Moore, "Is 'Existence' a Predicate?" in *The Ontological Argument*, ed. A. Plantinga (Garden City, N.Y., 1965), pp. 71ff.
23. Moore, ibid., pp. 74–75.
24. Moore, ibid., pp. 75–76.

It is not clear to me that in these examples Moore has noted any significant differences between "exists" and other properties, or at least any which are relevant to the ontological proof. If, by including fictional or imaginary tigers in our universe of discourse, we can give a sense to "Some tame tigers do not exist," then by the same device we can surely give a sense to "All tame tigers exist" and "Most tame tigers exist." Moreover, it is misleading of Moore to imply that when we do employ such a universe of discourse, we are changing the meaning of the word "exist" or indeed doing anything at all that has any special connection with the property of existence. We could just as well extend our universe of discourse in the same way for sentences like "Some tame tigers growl" and other sentences not involving the predicate of existence. Just how natural this would be depends on the context. If I say "Some cowboy heroes had white horses" it seems natural, in view of the cultural context of my remark, to include fictional cowboy heroes as well as real ones within the scope of the subject term. In other cases, this would be much less natural. It is true, as Moore observes, that such an understanding is positively *required* by "Some cowboy heroes existed, and some didn't." And this fact may perhaps indicate a significant difference between *exists* and other predicates. But it is not at all obvious that this difference does anything to show that existence cannot be included in the concept of a thing, or that all existential propositions must be synthetic. Perhaps the Kantian thesis is rendered more plausible by the fact that there are idioms like "There are tame tigers" as paraphrases for "Some tame tigers exist." For there is no natural idiom of this sort to paraphrase "Some tame tigers growl"; and the idiom itself—lacking as it does the same straightforward subject-predicate form, might lend support to the idea that when we say "X exists" we are saying something whose deeper logical form (as opposed to its surface grammatical form) is not that of a subject-predicate assertion. But the existence of such idioms surely constitutes no real argument for Kant's view.

The considerations which philosophers have advanced in favor of the Kantian position on existence and predication all strike me as extremely weak. As far as I can see, the principal reason why some philosophers have accepted this position is that once we do accept it, we have some plausible-sounding reason to give for rejecting the ontological proof, and therefore just possibly some means of freeing ourselves from the horrible nagging suspicion that this proof might be sound. And there can be no doubt that this has to be a strong recommendation for the Kantian position as far as many philosophers are concerned. But it can hardly be expected to make much impression on a convinced Cartesian.

Another Means of Escape

Not everyone who has rejected the ontological proof has found it necessary to adopt the Kantian view about existence and predication. Descartes' contemporary Caterus, for example, seems to have held both that existence is a perfection and that necessary existence is contained in the concept of a supremely perfect being, or is implied by its very name. Yet he found Descartes' *Meditations V* proof unconvincing:

> Even if it is granted that the very name of a being of highest perfection implies its existence, it still does not follow that this existence itself is something actual *in rerum natura*, but only that the concept of existence is inseparably conjoined with the concept of a highest being. From this you cannot infer that the existence of God is something actual, unless you suppose that such a highest being actually exists. For then it will possess all perfections along with the one of real existence.[25]

In this passage, Caterus admits that the proposition "God exists" is analytic (to put the admission in Kantian terminology). Yet he denies that we are entitled to conclude from this that God actually exists, unless we already suppose that he does. It appears to be Caterus' view that nothing can be truly predicated of a subject (even by means of an analytic proposition or an outright tautology) unless the subject exists. Such a view might well follow from the idea, which we have seen in Kant, that in a subject-predicate proposition the subject term is used to pick out something or other, and the predicate term is used to say something about the thing picked out. In order to say something true

25. Descartes, *Oeuvres*, 7:99; *Philosophical Works*, 2:7.

using such a proposition, both terms must succeed in doing their jobs. Of course, the proposition is false if the predicate does not belong to or apply to the subject picked out. But on this view, the proposition would also fail to be true if the subject term failed to refer to anything. A proponent of this view need not hold that in the latter event the proposition would be false. He might hold this, or he might deny any truth value at all to it. (In Caterus' Objections, I can find no indication of his view on this point.)

One possible disadvantage of Caterus' position is that it requires us to deny truth to such propositions as "A unicorn has one horn" and "Six-headed lions are six-headed," to analytic propositions whose subject terms happen not to refer to anything actual. The view might be rescued from this difficulty by permitting the reference of subject terms to include imaginary or fictional entities, and possessors of other nonreal modes of being. Caterus does not seem to permit this, however, and as we shall see presently, his criticism of the ontological argument would lose some of its force if he were to take a softer line on this point. When we consider propositions like "A unicorn has one horn," therefore, the Kantian way of escape from the ontological argument seems preferable to Caterus' way. For it saves the truth of analytic propositions about nonexistent things. On the other hand, as Caterus points out, we can form the concept "existent lion" and from it arrive at the analytic proposition "An existent lion exists," but we are not tempted to regard this as an a priori proof for the existence of lions. Caterus' view seems to explain better than Kant's why this should be so. For Kant must deal with the matter by altogether denying the legitimacy of concepts like "existent lion," and in the absence of a really convincing argument for his view about existence and predication, this seems somewhat arbitrary. Each way of escape from the ontological argument therefore has its advantages, and also its problems.

These two ways of escaping from the ontological argument are quite independent. Either may be adopted without the other, or both may be adopted at once. There is, in fact, good evidence that Kant himself endorsed Caterus' criticism of the ontological argument as well as the "Kantian" one. Probably the most explicit statement of this criticism is to be found in Kant's *Nova dilucidatio* essay of 1755. At that time, Kant had evidently not yet completely worked out his more radical criticism of the ontological proof, based on his view about existence and predication, and so drew his criticism of it from considerations very much along the same lines as Caterus':

> I know, of course, that appeal is made [by some philosophers] to the notion of God itself, who postulate that existence is determined in this notion. But it is easy to see that this may be done with truth only ideally, and not really. You form for yourself the notion of a being in which there is an *omnitudo realitatis*. And it must be admitted that according to this concept existence must belong to this being. The argument, therefore, proceeds thus: if in some being all realities without degree are united, that being exists; if they are conceived as united, existence follows, but only existence in idea. Hence the proposition may be formed thus: In forming for ourselves the notion of that which we call God, we have so determined it that existence is included in it. If then this preconceived notion be true, God exists. Only this much may be said in behalf of those who assent to the Cartesian argument.[26]

In this passage, Kant appears to concede that existence is a reality and hence that it may be found among the contents of the concept of an *ens realissimum*. His objection, like Caterus', is to the inference from this to the conclusion that an *ens realissimum* exists *realiter*. All we are entitled to infer, he says, is that such a being exists *idealiter* or "in idea."

H. J. Paton notes that in the *Critique* Kant often suggests that even analytic judgments are assumed to be about *objects*, and not merely about concepts, and Paton views this as an instance of Kant's unwavering belief that the truth of a proposition is always its correspondence with an object.[27] Such a view, of course, suggests that the subject term of even an analytic proposition must succeed in referring to an object if that proposition is to be counted as true. Kant even seems to be criticizing the ontological argument from this standpoint in one passage. If, he

26. *Gesammelte Schriften*, 1:394f; cf. England, *Kant's Conception of God*, pp. 223f.
27. H. J. Paton, *Kant's Metaphysic of Experience* (London, 1936) 1:214, fn. 3.

says, the proposition "this or that thing exists" is taken to be analytic, then "The assertion of the thing's existence adds nothing to the thought of the thing. But then either the thought which is in you is the thing itself, or else you have presupposed an existence as belonging to possibility, and then on the basis of the assertion you have inferred that existence from its inner possibility—which is nothing but a wretched tautology."[28] Kant's line in this passage seems to be that if any proposition of the form "X exists" is taken to be analytic *and true*, then the existence of some referent or other for its subject concept has already been presupposed. Either this referent must be regarded as the thought of this concept existing in someone's mind (a highly unnatural way to understand such a proposition, and clearly not what the proponent of the ontological argument means by it), or else it must be presupposed that some object corresponding to the subject concept actually exists in order that this reference may be secured. In the latter case, of course, the ontological argument would be flatly question-begging.

Kant's adherence to the view that every true predication requires the actual existence of some referent of the subject term also helps to make sense of some other things he says in this section of the *Critique*. Immediately after he states his views that "being" is not a real predicate, but only "the positing of a thing or of certain determinations," he proceeds to expound this view as follows: "The proposition: *God is omnipotent* contains two concepts, which have their objects: *God* and *omnipotence*. The little word *is* is not still another predicate over and above this, but only that which the predicate posits *in relation* to the subject."[29] It is tempting (and I believe in the end correct) to dismiss these remarks about the copulative "is" as irrelevant to the ontological argument, which after all has to do not with the use of the verb "to be" in which it serves to connect the subject with other predicates, but the use in which it (allegedly) serves as a full-fledged predicate all by itself. But what the passage indicates is that for Kant the copulative "is," like the "is" which simply asserts exis-

28. *Critique of Pure Reason*, A 597/B 625.
29. *Critique of Pure Reason*, A 598/B 626.

tence of its subject, has the function of "positing" something in the real world as standing over against our concepts. For Kant, the "exists" in "God exists" adds no predicate to the subject, but only "posits" an object corresponding to the subject concept. Likewise, the copula in "God is omnipotent" "posits" the real property of omnipotence in its relation to the subject of the proposition. To "posit" something, here as before, must mean to assert the extramental existence of an object corresponding to our concept of it. The copulative "is," therefore, must assert the actual existence of a property (e.g. omnipotence), standing in the categorical relation of inherence to the subsisting subject (God). But of course an actual property cannot inhere in a subject unless the subject also actually exists. Existing omnipotence can only inhere in an existing omnipotent thing. Hence Kant's view about the "positing" function of the copulative "is" seems to commit him to Caterus' view that every true predication presupposes the actual existence of that to which the subject term refers.

The Cartesian Reply

When Gassendi hints at the Kantian criticism of his *Meditations V* proof by asserting that existence is not a perfection, Descartes' only response is impatience:

> Here I do not see what genus of things you want existence to be in, nor do I see why it may not be said to be a property just as well as omnipotence, taking the term 'property' to include any attribute or anything which may be predicated of a thing, as it must be taken here. Indeed, necessary existence is a true property of God in the strictest sense, in that it belongs to him alone and makes up part of his essence alone.[30]

This reply, of course, would not be adequate to Kant's more fully worked-out view, which also challenges Descartes' claim here that existence is predicated of things in the fullest and strictest sense. But it seems to me that even the Kantian version of the criticism would be unable to shake his faith in the ontological proof unless this thesis about existence and predication

30. *Oeuvres*, 7:382f; *Philosophical Works*, 2:228.

could be supported by stronger arguments than those Kant actually supplies.

By contrast to his curt treatment of Gassendi's objection, however, Descartes shows considerable sympathy toward the views underlying Caterus' criticism. He agrees with Caterus that from the fact that a predicate P is stipulated to be part of the meaning of a subject term S (or, in more Kantian parlance, that the proposition "S is P" is analytic), it does not follow that S really is P. For Descartes, we can no more define a being into existence than we can define a triangle into having more than 180 degrees in its interior angles. In particular, Descartes readily admits that we cannot infer God's existence merely from the fact that the name "God" implies that God exists. "For," he says, "the fact that a word signifies that something is so does not make it true."[31]

In Descartes' view, the crucial point in the Fifth Meditation proof is that the idea of God represents to us a "true and immutable nature," whereas a complex such as "existent lion" represents only an arbitrary synthesis formed by our minds. By analyzing the latter sort of notion, we can get nothing but what we have "fictitiously" put into it. The idea of a true and immutable nature, however, presents us with a real synthesis of properties which necessarily belong together in the nature of things: "Not that my thought can bring it about [that God exists], or impose any necessity on things; but on the contrary, because the necessity which lies in the thing itself, that is, the necessary existence of God, determines me to this thought."[32] The analysis of such natures therefore supplies us with genuine knowledge of extramental reality.

Hence for Descartes from the fact that "S is P" is an analytic proposition, we *can* infer that S really is P, but only if S signifies a true and immutable nature and P can be clearly perceived by the mind to pertain to that nature. Descartes realizes that we may be wary of his proof because we are unaccustomed to distinguishing true and immutable natures from arbitrary mental

31. *Oeuvres*, 7:115; *Philosophical Works*, 2:19.
32. *Oeuvres*, 7:67; *Philosophical Works*, 1:181.

fictions, and because we are used to thinking about things whose nature involves only possible or contingent existence, and not about the one supremely perfect nature to which alone unconditionally necessary existence pertains. Nevertheless, Descartes insists, a careful inspection of our idea of a supremely perfect being reveals it to be the idea of a true and immutable nature, and moreover one to which the perfection of actual existence belongs.

Thus on Descartes' view from the analyticity. of "A white horse is white" we cannot infer a priori that any horse actually is white, because neither "horse" nor "white horse" names a true and immutable nature. Yet from the analyticity of "A triangle has its interior angles equal to two right angles" we can conclude that a triangle does have this property, because "triangle" names a true and immutable nature. This last, moreover, is a just conclusion even if there are no triangles or triangular shaped bodies actually existing. For in the case of true and immutable natures their essential attributes do actually pertain to them and can be truly predicated of them whether or not these natures are actually instantiated in anything having real or "formal" existence independent of our thought of them. Of course, we cannot infer the actual existence of a triangle (or of anything else, except a supremely perfect being) from its true and immutable nature, because it can be only possible or contingent existence which pertains to such natures.

For Descartes, then, the fact that "An existent lion exists" is an analytic proposition does not entitle us to infer the actual existence of any lion, because both "lion" and "existent lion" name the objects of adventitious or merely factitious ideas. The analyticity of the proposition "God exists," however, does entitle us to infer the actual existence of God, because "God" or "supremely perfect being" names a true and immutable nature to which actual existence necessarily pertains.

It is evident, then, that in the case of true and immutable natures Descartes does not accept the principle that every true predication presupposes the existence of what is referred to by the subject term. I believe Anthony Kenny is right when he suggests that such natures have for Descartes a kind of nonreal ontological status, neutral as between existence and nonexistence; that they are "given" to thought even when they do not "exist" in the extramental world.[33] Following certain scholastics, Descartes ascribes a kind of "objective being" to such natures, as intentional objects of thought. And the point of introducing such objects in the *Meditations V* is to point out that true predications can be made by using them as the referents of subject terms.[34] Of course, Descartes does not mean to identify these objects with our thoughts themselves, which in his view are actually existing modes of a thinking substance. The constitution of a true and immutable nature is, for him, in no way dependent on any (finite) mind, and the predicates which pertain to such natures would still have pertained to them necessarily even if they had never been thought of by us.

Now we can see why Caterus' criticism of the ontological argument would be weakened if he were to allow the referents of subject terms in true predication to include fictional or other nonreal things. Descartes might still agree with him in the case of objects which are strictly speaking fictional, that is, arbitrarily invented by our minds. (Descartes never indicates whether he would count "A unicorn has one horn" and other analytic propositions about purely fictional entities as true, or on what basis he would decide such questions). But once the door has been opened to true predications about nonreal objects, Descartes would be quick to insist that many truths of mathematics and metaphysics, those ascribing the pertinent predicates to true and immutable natures, must be admitted in this category.

Yet we may still wonder whether this would really be sufficient to establish the validity of the ontological proof for God's existence. William Alston apparently thinks not.[35] In his view,

33. Kenny, *Descartes* (New York, 1968) p. 155.

34. "And what is most to be considered here is that I find in myself innumerable ideas of certain things which, although they may well have existence nowhere outside me, still cannot be said to be nothing; and which, although it is up to my choice whether they are thought of, are still not just imagined (*finguntur*) by me, but have their own true and immutable natures. . . . And I can . . . demonstrate various properties of them" (*Oeuvres*, 7:64f; *Philosophical Works*, 1:179f).

35. William Alston, "The Ontological Argument Revisited," *The Ontological Argument*, pp. 86ff.

there is nothing wrong with according truth to predications about imaginary, fictional, or nonreal objects; but he denies that such predications can have any consequences of the sort alleged by Descartes for actually existing things. Alston distinguishes two ways in which a fictional or nonreal thing may be related to something real. In the first way, the nonreal thing may be the object of real thoughts, images, and so on, in someone's mind. Alston calls any such real mental thing the "real correlate" of the nonreal object. Secondly, we might specify "something which really exists and has all the characteristics (excluding existence, if that exclusion is necessary) of the nonreal existent." And this he calls the "real archetype" of the nonreal thing.[36] If, for example, I am thinking of a fictional character (say Ivan Karamazov), then the real correlate of what I am thinking of would be the thoughts I am having. The real archetype on the other hand, would be an actual human being, who lived in Russia in the nineteenth century, who went insane at his half-brother's trial for patricide, and so on.

According to Alston, "it seems to be a defining feature of all nonreal modes of existence that any statement about something which exists in such a mode will have no implications with respect to real things, except for its real correlate and any implications that might have. In particular it has no implications concerning its real archetype."[37] What Alston says here does seem to be true for statements which are about imaginary, dreamt of or fictional entities. Once we accept the *Brothers Karamazov* as a *fictional* narrative, nothing that is said in it about Ivan Karamazov can have any direct implication for any actual person who might happen to resemble this creation of Dostoyevsky's imagination. Even if, by the author's biographical intent or by an astonishing coincidence, there did actually live in Russia in the nineteenth century a man named Ivan Karamazov who did all the things ascribed to the character in Dostoyevsky's novel, nothing Dostoyevsky wrote in a work of fiction could be taken to have a direct implication about this real archetype of his fic-

36. Ibid., p. 103.
37. Ibid., pp. 103f.

tional character. This fact is, I believe, as Alston holds, a defining feature of fictional or imaginative modes of discourse.

But it is not so obvious that it is a defining feature of *every* mode of discourse about nonreal objects. In particular, it is not evident that it is a defining feature of modes of discourse about Cartesian true and immutable natures. Descartes strenuously denies, as we have seen, that such natures are imaginary or fictional entities, entities concocted by the human mind in the way that characters in a novel are. Descartes holds that "A triangle has its three interior angles equal to two right angles" is a true proposition even if there do not exist *in rerum natura* any triangles or triangular objects. For this reason, he holds that the referent of the subject term of this proposition is something "given" to thought even if no such referent actually exists. But he also believes that the truth of this proposition has some very direct implications for the real archetypes of the nonreal object which the proposition is about, that is, for any triangles or triangular objects which happen to exist in the real world. Specifically, Descartes believes that the truth of this proposition about a nonreal object implies that any triangles or triangular objects which exist in the real world will necessarily have their interior angles equal to two right angles. This belief, moreover, seems to be a perfectly reasonable one. It points in addition to a crucial distinction between Cartesian natures and merely fictional objects. It is a defining feature of discourse about fictional objects not only that they may possess properties that nothing does in fact have, but also that they may possess properties which it is impossible for anything to have. In such a narrative, a clever and mathematically minded author (such as Lewis Carroll) might very well concoct a convincing fantasy in which some fictional triangle has its interior angles unequal to two right angles. No twisting and turning of the human imagination, however, could alter the essential properties of a true and immutable nature.

Alston is especially wary, of course, of the possible implications of nonreal things with respect to the existence of their real archetypes. He writes: "If the existence of something in one mode should imply its existence in another mode, the distinction between the two modes would crumble."[38] What Alston apparently fears is that if some property of an imagined or fictional object should imply the actual existence of its real archetype, then the distinction between discourse about fictional objects and discourse about real ones would break down. But we ought not to fear this in the same way in the case of discourse about Cartesian true and immutable natures. For discourse about such nonreal entities does have implications for any real archetypes of these entities there happen to be, without threatening the distinction between them. The point of discourse about true and immutable natures is to furnish us with knowledge which holds good *whether or not* there exist real archetypes of the nonreal objects of that knowledge. It is true that in the case of a necessarily existent being, the distinction between real and nonreal natures, or the distinction between discourse about such natures and discourse about their real archetypes, does crumble away. But this is only to say that this nature does exist necessarily. Of course there is still room for distinguishing between the true and immutable nature of God, which necessarily exists, and merely fictional *realissima*, which may not, just as we can distinguish between the true and immutable nature of a triangle, which necessarily has the properties ascribed to it by the theorems of geometry, and merely fictional triangles, which may not have these properties.

All this presupposes, of course, that Descartes' theory of true and immutable natures gives the correct account of our mathematical and metaphysical knowledge. And obviously this presupposition is easy enough to challenge from a Kantian standpoint. The best Kantian analogues to Descartes' true and immutable natures are the objects of mathematics, such as numbers and geometrical figures, which may be exhibited a priori in the pure intuitions of space and time. Like the true and immutable natures of Descartes, they involve a necessary synthesis of different properties which we apprehend immediately a priori. Yet for Kant the concepts of such objects are not generated spon-

38. Ibid., p. 104.

taneously by the understanding; they are rather "constructed" from what is given in our pure, but always sensible, intuition. For Kant, our understanding provides merely the forms of synthesis or connection for data which must always be given (whether a priori or empirically) via sensibility. And the mathematical objects given us a priori in pure intuition can thus consist only in the spatio-temporal forms of phenomena, their geometric shapes, and the magnitudes of one kind or another which may be found in them. There can be no question, therefore, of any a priori construction of the concept of a supersensible object, such as a supremely perfect being. The idea of God could represent to us something like a true and immutable nature only if we possessed an intuitive understanding, a capacity to produce concepts wholly a priori without any reliance on sensibility to supply their contents.

The critical philosophy, therefore, involves epistemological restrictions which are sufficient to bar the way to any pretended intuition of the true and immutable nature of God, and thus to any ontological proof of the Cartesian type. Kant did not choose to combat the proof in this manner, however. Perhaps a criticism along these lines would have conceded too much to the ontological proof for his taste, by suggesting that it might well succeed in the context of a more rationalistic epistemology. Such a suggestion, however, is very likely correct. After all, it is plausible to think that philosophers of the caliber of Descartes, Spinoza, Malebranche, and Leibniz would not have unanimously concluded that the proof followed from their principles unless it really did follow from them. In any case, I cannot help feeling that a criticism of the Cartesian proof founded straightforwardly on Kant's epistemology would have been far more compelling than the famous but badly underargued one actually presented in the *Critique*.

The Cosmological Proof

As we noted earlier, Kant divides the cosmological proof into two stages, the first establishing the existence of a necessary being and the second showing this being to be an *ens realis-simum*. In fact, he finds neither stage persuasive, but grants the first stage for the sake of argument in order to concentrate on the second. His aim is to show that this stage is covertly dependent on the ontological argument he has just criticized.

Kant says that the ontological proof "secretly underlies" the cosmological and is "presupposed" by it. The cosmological proof, he asserts, is no more than "an old argument disguised as a new one." "It is really only the ontological proof from mere concepts which is contained in the so-called cosmological power of proof."[39] Such remarks strongly suggest that Kant believes the ontological proof to be contained in the cosmological as a sort of tacit premise. And they further suggest that he regards this tacit premise as doing all the work, so that the appeal to experience (to the existence of the finite self, or of a contingent world in general) is in fact superfluous, merely an empty gesture.

Perhaps Kant did think these things. But his actual criticism of the cosmological proof makes no real case for them, nor does it even try to do so. In particular, Kant does not maintain that the appeal to experience is superfluous in the argument's first stage. This appeal, he admits, "serves, perhaps, to lead us to the concept of absolute necessity, but not to establish this concept as pertaining to any determinate thing. For as soon as this is our intention, we must immediately leave all experience behind and seek among pure concepts for those which contain the possibility of an absolutely necessary being."[40] Kant's claim, then, is only that if we accept the inference from necessary existence to supreme reality in the proof's second stage, then we are committed to accepting the ontological argument. All a priori theistic proofs, he says, proceed in one of two ways: "either to find a way from absolute necessity to its concept, or a way from the concept of some thing or other to the absolute necessity of that thing. If we can do the one, then we must be able to do the

39. *Critique of Pure Reason*, A 606/B 634; above, p. 73.
40. *Gesammelte Schriften*, 28, 2, 2, pp. 1030f; *Lectures on Philosophical Theology*, p. 62.

other."[41] Thus Kant's criticism of the cosmological proof is not that the ontological serves it as a tacit premise, but rather that if we assume that the cosmological proof works, then we are committed to holding that the ontological argument works as well. The idea is that since the ontological proof has already shown itself to be unsound, any proof which is found to be committed to it must be equally unsound. If Kant's claim can be made out, this would certainly be an effective attack on the cosmological proof, assuming, of course, that his earlier criticism of the ontological proof was successful.

The second stage of the cosmological proof must show that the necessary being whose existence has been demonstrated in the first stage is a supremely real being, and it has the concept of necessary existence in general from which to derive this conclusion. Consequently, according to Kant, it must argue that the concept of supreme reality alone is adequate to the concept of necessary existence, so that every necessary being *eo ipso* has to be an *ens realissimum*. How does Kant think the second stage of the cosmological proof infers supreme reality from absolute necessity?

This argument runs as follows: A necessary being can only be determined in one way: that is, with respect to all possible *praedicatorum contradictoria oppositorum* it must be determined by one of these opposed predicates. Consequently, it must be thoroughly determined by its concept. But there is only one possible concept of a thing which determines it thoroughly a priori, and this is the concept of an *entis realissimi*. For in every possible pair of *praedicatis contradictorie oppositis*, only the reality always belongs to it. Or in other words, there exists an *ens realissimum* and it exists necessarily.[42]

The argument here is obscure, though the influence of Kant's possibility proof is quite evident. There is no need to look too closely at the argument, however, since Kant's purpose is precisely to show that its inference from necessary existence to supreme reality cannot be validly drawn. Kant takes the general

41. *Critique of Pure Reason*, A 612/B 641.
42. *Gesammelte Schriften*, 28, 2, 2, p. 1030; *Lectures on Philosophical Theology*, p. 61; cf. *Critique of Pure Reason*, A 605/B 633f.

principle of the inference, that every necessary being is supremely real, and argues that it, like any universal affirmative
judgment, is convertible *per accidens*, so that a particular judgment of the converse form may be derived from it. From "All
crows are black," I may infer "Some black thing is a crow." In
a like manner, argues Kant, from "All necessary beings are supremely real," I may infer "Some supremely real being is a
necessary being." But, Kant points out, the concept of a supremely real being is completely determined with respect to
every pair of contradictory predicates; its concept is therefore
not a universal concept but a Leibnizian complete notion, the
concept of an individual thing. Such a concept, however, is not
a concept which can be applied to more than one being. (The
argument here, of course, rests on another Leibnizian principle:
the identity of indiscernibles). From the complete determination
of the concept of an *ens realissimum*, Kant thus infers that "what
is valid of *some* under this concept, is also valid of *all*. Hence I
will be able (in this case) also to convert the proposition *absolutely*, i.e., every most real being is a necessary being; . . . which
is just to assert the ontological proof."[43]

A number of critics have taken issue with Kant's inference
here from "All necessary beings are supremely real" to "Some
supremely real being is a necessary being." Such a conversion
per accidens, they insist, is not valid when the universal proposition converted is not taken to have "existential import."[44] To
take J. J. C. Smart's example, when we assert that all trespassers
will be prosecuted, we do not necessarily mean to say that there
ever will be trespassers, but only that if there are any, then they
will be prosecuted. And from such an assertion we are not
entitled to infer that someone who will be prosecuted is a tres-
passer, unless we suppose in addition that at least one trespas-
ser actually exists. Kant's conversion *per accidens* of "All neces-

43. *Critique of Pure Reason*, A 608/B 636; cf. *Gesammelte Schriften*, 28, 2, 2,
p. 1031; *Lectures on Philosophical Theology*, p. 62.

44. See Fr. T. A. Johnson, "A Note on Kant's Criticism of the Arguments for
the Existence of God," *Australasian Journal of Philosophy* 21 (1943), 13; D. J. B.
Hawkins, *Essentials of Theism* (New York, 1949), pp. 67–70; J. J. C. Smart, "The
Existence of God," in *The Cosmological Arguments*, ed. Donald R. Burrill (Garden
City, N.Y., 1967), pp. 266f.

sary beings are supremely real" is therefore valid only if he already presupposes the existence of a necessary being. But, the critics insist, this presupposition is not justified unless one grants the validity of the cosmological proof, which it is precisely Kant's purpose to dispute.

I wholly agree with Peter Remnant, however, who holds that these criticisms of Kant are quite beside the point.[45] For in Kant's behalf it may be replied that of course he *does* suppose, in his conversion *per accidens* of "All necessary beings are supremely real," that there does exist at least one necessary being. And he is fully entitled to do so, since he has granted for the sake of argument that the existence of such a being has been demonstrated by the first stage of the cosmological proof. Surely the proponent of the proof is in no position to dispute this presupposition, since it is drawn from his own argument. Hence he is in no position to refute the inference Kant means to draw on the basis of it.

Kant's critics at this point are misled, I believe, because they take Kant to be arguing that the ontological proof serves as a tacit premise in the cosmological, giving the latter proof all its strength and reducing the appeal to experience in the first stage to a mere sham. Hence they are quick to point out that Kant is able to "uncover" the ontological argument only if he presupposes that the existence of a necessary being has been proven independently. This would certainly be enough to explode the idea that the cosmological proof succeeds in demonstrating the existence of a necessary being only by smuggling in the ontological as a tacit premise. But as we have seen, Kant's criticism of the cosmological argument does not in fact aim at substantiating this idea. Rather it seeks only to show that if we suppose the cosmological argument to be sound, then we must suppose the ontological argument to be sound too. Nothing in this claim requires Kant to treat the first stage of the cosmological argument as superfluous to the argument as a whole, or to deny that it establishes the existence of a necessary being in a manner independent of the ontological.

45. Peter Remnant, "Kant and the Cosmological Argument," *The First Critique*, pp. 143–146.

Kant is therefore quite correct, it seems to me, in holding that anyone who believes that every necessary being is supremely real is committed to the converse of this, that every supremely real being exists necessarily. For this follows inevitably, granted only that we realize the uniqueness of the concept of a supremely real being, and accept the Leibnizian principle of the identity of indiscernibles. But in spite of this I do not think he succeeds in showing that the acceptance of the cosmological proof commits one to accepting the ontological. The problem is not with the inference we have just been examining, but with the interpretation of its conclusion.

According to Kant, the proposition "Every supremely real being exists necessarily" amounts to the ontological proof for God's existence. But does it? Whether it does seems to depend, to begin with, on what we mean by "exists necessarily." If the proposition "Every supremely real being exists necessarily" is to amount to the ontological argument, then it will have to be construed as saying that "A supremely real being exists" is a necessary truth, and presumably an analytic proposition, one whose predicate is contained in the concept of its subject. In other words, it will have to construe the phrase "necessary existence" to mean *logically* necessary existence. But the meaning of this phrase must be determined by the sort of necessary existence which has (supposedly) been demonstrated in the first stage of the cosmological proof. The question then is whether this sort of necessary existence has to be taken as logically necessary existence.

The first stage of the cosmological proof argues for the existence of a being not causally dependent on anything else, or requiring anything else as a causal condition for its existence. Many rationalists did apparently identify God's causal or metaphysical necessity with logical necessity. For they held that God's existence is causally independent of anything else because God contains the ground of his existence in himself; and they attributed this to the fact that existence belongs among the perfections constituting God's essence. Such philosophers, of course, were usually explicit supporters of the ontological proof and would not have been in the least embarrassed to learn that they were committed to it by their conception of God's necessary existence. The question, however, is whether the cosmological proof by itself requires such a conception.

In both the *Critique* and the *Lectures on Philosophical Theology*, Kant claims that any concept of necessary existence is *eo ipso* a concept of logically necessary existence. "For," he says, "reason recognizes that only as absolutely necessary which is necessary from its concept."[46] Yet it is hard to see how Kant can expect us to credit this statement. For he himself claimed in the *Beweisgrund* essay to have formulated a concept of necessary existence which differs from the concept of logically necessary existence used in the ontological proof. Quite apart from this, it seems possible to reject the idea of logically necessary existence altogether (as Kant does) and still to hold that there is a being which causes all others while itself neither having nor requiring any causal conditions for its own existence. A being of this sort, however, is all that we are concerned with in the first stage of the cosmological proof.[47]

But even if we grant that "Every supremely real being exists necessarily," as it is understood in the cosmological argument, commits us to regarding "God exists" as an analytic proposition, it still does not follow that accepting the cosmological proof commits us to accepting the ontological. For as we saw earlier, Caterus believed that "God exists" is an analytic proposition, but rejected the ontological proof because he held that every true predication, even in an analytic proposition, presupposes the existence of the referent of its subject term. All a proponent of the cosmological proof need do to escape the ontological proof is to agree with Caterus' criticism of it. And once again, Kant is in no position to bar his way, since Caterus' criticism

46. *Critique of Pure Reason*, A 612/B 640.
47. Such a conception of "causally necessary existence" has been ably defended by Alvin Plantinga in "Necessary Being," *The Cosmological Arguments*, pp. 125–141. Jonathan Bennett (*Kant's Dialectic*, pp. 252ff) remains unpersuaded by Kant's attempt to reduce the ontological proof to the cosmological, but he finds more convincing what he calls Kant's "radical criticism" of the cosmological argument, "its tolerating the notion of logically necessary existence." Yet if in fact the proponent of the cosmological proof need not tolerate this notion, then the "radical criticism" also fails.

is one Kant himself endorsed. Even Descartes, as we also saw, did not draw his ontological proof simply from the analyticity of "God exists"; he apparently agreed with Caterus that the analyticity of this proposition alone (without the intellectual perception of supreme perfection as a true and immutable nature) does not justify our predicating existence of a supremely perfect being. Hence to reason, as Kant does, from the second stage of the cosmological proof to the ontological proof is to reason in a way which even Descartes would have regarded as fallacious.

The Physicotheological Proof

Kant's Critique of the Proof

The cosmological proof argues from the contingent existence of a world in general to the necessary existence of a supremely perfect being as its cause or sufficient ground. The physicotheological proof argues from the specific constitution of the actual world. More concretely, as Kant understands the proof, it argues from the beauty and harmony of the natural world, the variety and order found in it, and the purposive arrangements which can be observed in natural things.[48] The natural theist claims that "this purposive order is wholly alien to the things of the world, and depends on them only contingently, i.e., the nature of various things of itself . . . could not have agreed to determinate final aims." From the analogy of natural purposes with those of human art, the theist then concludes that the cause of nature's order is very probably a rational intelligence, possessed of great wisdom, directing things to their ends by free will. "The unity of this cause may be inferred from the unity of the reciprocal reference of the parts of the world as elements of an artfully contrived structure."[49]

In the *Critique of Pure Reason*, Kant approaches this proof as he did the cosmological, distinguishing in it a first stage, which attempts to justify our assigning an intelligent cause for nature's order, and a second stage whose task is to show that this cause

48. *Critique of Pure Reason*, A 622/B 650.
49. *Critique of Pure Reason*, A 625/B 653.

is an *ens realissimum*. As before, he concedes the first stage of the proof for the sake of argument, and concentrates on the second. Granting that the order in nature is strong evidence for the existence of a wise designer of that order, he contends that it is still insufficient to give us any determinate concept of this intelligent cause, and in particular that it can never justify a belief in a supremely real being. For the latter is an idea of reason, and no experience can ever be adequate to it. From the wondrous and immeasurably great order in the world, I may be able to infer an extremely wise and resourceful designer of that order, but not one possessed of metaphysically infinite or ontologically supreme degree of intelligence and power. Hence the natural theist who is seeking a proof for the existence of an *ens realissimum* must leave behind his empirical evidence at this point and fall into a purely transcendental inference to complete his proof.

Thus the argument based on empirical grounds is suddenly abandoned, and we proceed from the contingency of the world which was inferred at the beginning from its order and purposiveness. From this contingency alone we now go, solely by means of transcendental concepts, to the existence of something absolutely necessary, and from the absolute necessity of this first cause to its completely determined (or determining) concept, namely that of an all-inclusive reality. Hence the physicotheological proof, when it gets stuck in its undertaking escapes this embarrassment by leaping suddenly to the cosmological proof. And since the latter is only a hidden ontological proof, it actually fulfills its intention merely through pure reason.[50]

This may perhaps be an accurate reconstruction of the manner in which some theists in fact have argued (in particular, it is not an unfair account of Kant's own highly sympathetic representation of the physicotheological argument in Part One, Section Three of the *Lectures on Philosophical Theology*).[51] But regarded as a reconstruction of empirical theism generally, it is arbitrary and unpersuasive. Kant was induced to give such an account, one supposes, principally by his desire to find in physicotheol-

50. *Gesammelte Schriften*, 28, 2, 2, pp. 1007–1009; *Lectures on Philosophical Theology*, pp. 36–38; *Critique of Pure Reason*, A 621/B 649, A 629/B 657.
51. *Gesammelte Schriften*, 28, 2, 2, pp. 1062ff; *Lectures on Philosophical Theology*, pp. 99ff.

ogy a covert reliance on the cosmological argument, paralleling the alleged dependence of the latter on the ontological proof. But he makes no real case at all that physicotheology, by its very nature, involves any hidden dependence on, or even a commitment to, any a priori arguments. The very most Kant might hope to show is that the existence of an *ens realissimum* cannot be established without relying on arguments a priori.

It is doubtful, however, that any convinced empirical theist would be greatly disturbed by this result. A natural theist who altogether repudiated the ontological and cosmological proofs in favor of the physicotheological proof might very well likewise repudiate the metaphysical concept of an *ens realissimum* in favor of some less rationalistic conception of nature's author. Hume's Cleanthes, for example, maintains that the order and purposive arrangements in the natural world constrain us to regard the cause of the world as an intelligent being, something like the human mind but far surpassing it in wisdom and power. Not only is he quite content with this "indeterminate" concept of God, but he altogether rejects, as incomprehensible, mystical, and even "atheistic," the notions of infinite perfection and necessary existence which lie at the foundation of rationalist theology.[52]

Physicotheology as Moral Faith and Natural Science

Kant's official criticism of the physicotheological approach in the *Critique of Pure Reason* actually gives us a very poor idea of his extremely complex attitude toward physicotheology. This attitude was in certain respects one of great sympathy, and in others of extreme suspicion. The whole strategy of Kant's criticism of the three theistic proofs is based on the idea that all three in the end reduce to the ontological proof, "The only possible ground of proof with which human reason can never dispense."[53] From this point of view, the physicotheological proof, the one farthest from this pure rational ground, must also be regarded as the least rationally transparent. Yet according to Kant the physicotheological proof "always deserves to be men-

52. Hume, *Dialogues concerning Natural Religion*, p. 32.
53. *Critique of Pure Reason*, A 625/B 653.

tioned with respect. It is the oldest, clearest, and best adapted to common human reason."[54] Kant's respect for physicotheology derives from what he took to be its unique value for morality and moral religion, as well as from what he believed was its indispensable contribution to the empirical science of nature.

Moral faith, in Kant's view, is the attitude of the moral man toward the order of the world in which he must direct his action toward the realization of the highest good. Through his trust in a wise author of nature, the rational agent renders conceivable the possibility of this final end, and avoids the moral despair in which the course of the world often threatens to engulf his moral disposition. The ultimate wisdom of providence, of course, is not something in Kant's view which any finite being can expect to verify, or even fully to comprehend. Nevertheless, since the moral man believes in the governance of the world by a supremely wise plan, it is only natural that he should be on the lookout for signs of this wisdom, and that he should find in the purposive arrangements he observes in the natural world an apparent confirmation of his morally grounded convictions. The physicotheological proof, therefore, is in common thinking very closely allied to moral faith, and is often innocently confused with it.[55] Kant emphasizes that this is no real support for the physicotheological proof itself, regarded purely as a theoretical argument. But it is apparently the principal reason why Kant thought the argument from design was deservedly the most persuasive to the common man of the three traditional theistic proofs:

Hence the fact that the physicoteleological proof convinces just as if it were a theological proof, comes not from our use of the ideas of natural purposes as so many empirical grounds of proof for a highest understanding. Rather, it mixes itself unnoticed with the moral ground of proof, which dwells in every man and thus moves him most inwardly. . . . The physicotheological proof, however, has only the merit of leading the mind's consideration of the world onto the path of purposes and thus to an *intelligent* author of the world: And then the moral reference to purposes and the idea of a suitable legislator and author of the

54. *Critique of Pure Reason*, A 623/B 651.
55. See my *Kant's Moral Religion* (Ithaca, N.Y., 1970), pp. 171–176.

world as a theological concept appears to develop spontaneously out of the physicotheological ground of proof, although in fact it is a pure addition.[56]

But Kant also believed that physicotheology, if properly employed, is of genuine assistance to natural science in its task of discovering order, pattern, and regularity in experience. Physicotheology, he says "enlivens the study of nature. . . . It brings in purposes and intentions where our observation by itself would not have discovered them, and extends our knowledge of nature by providing the clue to a special unity whose principle is outside nature."[57]

The aim of natural science, as Kant conceives it, is to maximize unity and order in our empirical knowledge of the sensible world. In the Analogies of Experience, Kant tries to show that one species of order, that of universal causal mechanism, belongs necessarily and a priori to any possible experience. The principle of this causality is that the coming to be of every state of affairs in time is causally determined by some antecedent state of affairs according to a necessary rule or law. But the necessary order of causal mechanism is not the only sort of order thinkable in nature, nor indeed the only sort actually found in it. In the Appendix to the Dialectic of the *Critique of Pure Reason*, Kant discusses a wholly different kind of order found in nature by the mind; but he gives his definitive account of it only in the *Critique of Judgment*.

According to Kant, the order of the natural world consists not only in necessary causal sequences of events or states of affairs, but also in the existence of organized systems such as those found in the life processes of plants and animals. Such an organism or "organized being" is constituted by a contingent arrangement of causal conditions, which gives rise to a self-organizing, self-perpetuating, self-reproducing, or self-developing form or structure. In view of the intricate arrangement of natural processes in such a being, the subordination of each part or element to the organization of the whole, Kant calls an organized

56. *Gesammelte Schriften*, 5:477f; cf. *Critique of Judgment*, trans. J. H. Bernard (New York, 1951), pp. 330f.
57. *Critique of Pure Reason*, A 625/B 651.

being a "natural purpose" (*Naturzweck*). In such beings, according to him, we discover alongside the mechanistic order of nature an order of another sort. The ground of this order is not simply a necessary principle of abstract causal regularity, but the apparently contingent yet inherently stable structural pattern which is, in Kant's strikingly appropriate phrase, "both cause and effect of itself."[58]

The concept of an organized being or natural purpose is, in principle, a loose and flexible one. It is not a concept, in Kant's view, under which the mind can subsume data directly or immediately, through the faculty of "determining judgment." For in order to view something as part of a self-organizing or self-developing structure, we need first to come up with the concept of the particular structure with reference to which this judgment is made. The life-processes of plants and animals provide us with many different kinds of organized structures, each different from the rest. The discovery of purposive order in nature depends not on general features of organisms, but on a recognition of the particular structure appropriate to a given organism. For this reason the discovery of purposive order in nature requires a creative act of the mind, akin, in Kant's view, to artistic creation. It is a function of "reflective judgment," which does not merely *apply* a universal concept to a particular instance, but instead *discovers* the universal which best fits a given particular. The comprehension of this special kind of order in nature, in other words, depends on our ability to see such a structure in natural processes, and to find the concept which exactly captures the specific form of self-organization proper to it.

According to Kant, there are four conceivable ways in which we might try to account for the existence of natural purposes: (1) we might think of them as arising purely by chance from the operations of causal mechanisms. (2) We might regard them as resulting from some hidden principle of blind natural necessity. Or (3) we might suppose that matter as such contains "life" or self-organization as one of its inherent principles or essential capacities. Or, finally, (4) we might ascribe the intricate arrangement of natural purposes to the wise intentions of an intelligent

---

58. *Gesammelte Schriften*, 5:370; cf. *Critique of Judgment*, p. 217.

author of nature. Kant's names for these four hypotheses are, respectively: (1) Epicureanism, (2) Spinozism, (3) hylozoism, and (4) theism. Kant regards these four hypotheses as encompassing all conceivable explanations of natural purposiveness, by attributing it to (1) "lifeless matter," (2) a "lifeless God," (3) "living matter," or (4) "a living God." [59]

Kant does not think that we can decide "objectively" between these four hypotheses. As ways of explaining natural purposes, however, and making them intelligible to the human mind, he does not regard all four as equally satisfying. Epicureanism and Spinozism, in his view, do not so much attempt to explain the purposiveness in nature as to explain it *away*; the appearance of purpose, on these views, is something either fortuitous or inevitable, but is in no way "intentional." Kant describes these two hypotheses as an "idealism of purposiveness," meaning that for them the purposiveness of nature is nothing real, but only an illusion in the mind of the observer. [60] Hylozoism, by contrast, is treated by Kant as a "realism of purposiveness"; yet he regards its account of natural purposes also as inadequate. The only examples of matter endowed with life which the hylozoist can cite are precisely those living organisms whose curious purposive structure is in need of explanation. Hence "there must be a circle in the explanation if we would derive the natural purposiveness of organized beings from the life of matter." Besides, Kant asserts, the very concept of living matter is contradictory: "lifelessness, inertia, constitutes the essential character of matter." [61]

Neither does Kant seem to be entirely satisfied with theism as an explanation of natural purposiveness. And he is emphatic that we can never "dogmatically establish the theistic account as the objectively correct one." For we cannot, he says, demonstrate that purposive order could not have arisen solely through the natural mechanism. Nevertheless, owing to the "special constitution of my cognitive faculties" I can best make natural purposes intelligible to myself by thinking of them as intentional

---

59. *Gesammelte Schriften*, 5:389–91; cf. *Critique of Judgment*, pp. 236–39.
60. *Gesammelte Schriften*, 5:391; cf. *Critique of Judgment*, p. 238.
61. *Gesammelte Schriften*, 5:394; cf. *Critique of Judgment*, p. 242.

products of an intelligent being. For this reason, theism "has the advantage over all other grounds of explanation in that the understanding it ascribes to the original being best rescues the purposiveness of nature from idealism and introduces for its production an intentional causality." [62] The theistic view of nature thus provides us with a conception of natural purposiveness which is clear, simple, and well adapted to our faculties. Armed with it, we may more easily go out in search of that peculiar kind of order which organized beings exhibit. Theism, in Kant's view, therefore is of considerable heuristic value for empirical science.

The Weaknesses of Empirical Theism

Kant's reasons for singling out the theistic hypothesis in this way seem rather questionable. Does theism really represent natural purposes as more "real," or make them more inherently "intelligible" than the other hypotheses? Of course it does if we insist on taking the term "purpose" literally as implying a means-end connection which has to remain mysterious or dubious unless it is referred to the deliberate plan of some conscious agent. But none of the hypotheses, even the Epicurean, deny the *reality* of self-organizing structures in the natural world, any more than we need deny the reality of a royal flush in claiming that it resulted from a haphazard deal of the cards. Both Spinozism and hylozoism, by opening up the possibility that an apparently contingent or "voluntary" arrangement of matter may actually be a necessary phenomenon of nature, or result from the inherent properties of matter itself, would seem to make natural purposes more directly and essentially "explicable" than theism does.

Nor does Kant himself always eschew explanations of this sort for natural phenomena. First in the *Beweisgrund* essay and again in the *Lectures on Philosophical Theology*, he points out that some natural phenomena (such as the oblate shape of the earth) appear at first glance to be both contingent and to serve a purpose, but in fact result simply from the nature of matter. And he in-

62. *Gesammelte Schriften*, 5:397, 395, 398; cf. *Critique of Judgment*, pp. 244, 242, 245.

sists that all such phenomena must be explained by reference
to the necessary nature of the original being who produced it,
and cannot be ascribed to his free will.[63] Why does Kant feel so
free to adopt this hylozoist, or at least dangerously Spinozist,
line about some phenomena, while rejecting it as a possible explanation of natural purposes generally?

Both the Kantian conception of a natural purpose and the
Kantian version of the physicotheological argument are predicated on the assumption that there are many cases of self-organization in nature which we cannot account for by reference to
the inherent properties of matter itself. For Kant, of course, the
"properties of matter" included only those features belonging
directly to the causal mechanism set forth in a Newtonian
mathematical physics. Looking at the matter from this standpoint, it is obvious that the number of cases in which apparently
contingent purposive phenomena could be explained solely by
reference to such mechanical causes was bound to be very small.
Hence Kant must have regarded it both as extremely far-fetched
to suppose that every natural purpose can be explained in this
manner, and methodologically unwise to proceed as if such
explanations might be generally forthcoming.[64] Such an attitude
on his part might have been a sensible one in the days prior to
such "Epicurean" and "hylozoist" developments in biology as
the theory of natural selection and the discovery of DNA.

But this means that the concept of a natural purpose really
applies only to those phenomena of self-organization which
result from the (apparently) contingent arrangements of matter,
and not to those self-organizing structures which might be seen
to result from the properties found empirically to belong essentially to it. This seems to be the real reason why Kant is unsatis-

63. *Gesammelte Schriften*, 2:118ff; *Gesammelte Schriften*, 28, 2, 2, p. 1035; *Lectures on Philosophical Theology*, p. 67.

64. This view lies behind a famous passage from the *Critique of Judgment*: "It
is wholly certain that we cannot sufficiently acquaint ourselves with organized
beings and their inner possibility from merely mechanical principles of nature,
much less explain them. And with equal certainty we can say flatly that it is
unsuited to mankind to take up such a task or to hope that perhaps one day
there is going to arise a Newton who will make comprehensible the production
of a blade of grass from natural laws which no intention has ordered" (*Gesammelte Schriften*, 5:400; cf. *Critique of Judgment*, p. 248).

fied by Epicurean, Spinozist, and hylozoist explanation of natural purposiveness. It is also the reason why his version of the physicotheological argument boldly claims that "purposive order is wholly alien to the things of the world," and cannot be explained by the very nature of these things.

But a physicotheological proof based on this sort of argument is open to two serious dangers. First, it is just the sort of theistic argument which is in constant competition with natural science and lives essentially in the "gaps" of scientific explanation. As purely naturalistic or materialistic explanations of the phenomena of self-organization accumulate, and as the prospects for more of them increase, the case for theism derived from these sources becomes correspondingly weaker. Kant was not particularly worried by this danger to physicotheology, partly because he seems to have felt that there was little prospect of a convincing naturalistic explanation of biological phenomena generally, and partly because he believed he had found a way of viewing physicotheology which prevented it from being at loggerheads with empirical science. (We will be having a look at this part of his doctrine later.)

The second danger to physicotheology is one Kant saw quite clearly. Given a physicotheological proof drawn only from contingent forms of self-organization, and unexplainable by purely mechanical causes, "the purposiveness and harmony of so many natural structures can only prove the contingency of form, but not of matter, i.e., not of the substance of the world. . . . At most, therefore, the proof can establish only an *architect* of the world, who is always limited by the suitability of the raw materials with which he works. It cannot establish a *creator*, to whose idea everything is subject." [65] The natural theist's argument thus threatens to commit him to serious theological unorthodoxy, to a God who is author merely of the "forms" of things, and not the creator *ex nihilo* of the material world itself. [66] Of course the natural theist may reply that while his argument does not establish the claim that matter itself exists contingently and depends

65. *Critique of Pure Reason*, A 626f/B 654f.
66. *Gesammelte Schriften*, 28, 2, 2, p. 1093f; *Lectures on Philosophical Theology*, p. 133f.

on a creator, the argument may nevertheless be compatible with this claim. This is not so clear, however. For the physicotheological argument, as we have seen, presupposes a distinction between two sorts of phenomena: (1) those which the constitution of matter by itself can explain, and (2) the phenomena of contingent order and purpose, which require an intelligent designer as their only satisfactory explanation. But if after giving this argument we go on to insist that matter itself requires an intelligent being as its creator, then we seem to have altogether abolished the first category of phenomena. It now no longer makes any real difference whether the phenomena of self-organization result from the inherent properties of matter, or only from its contingent arrangement. For the creative intelligence of a Deity is required to account for matter in any case. The physicotheological argument can only appeal to us so long as we are willing to suppose (at least for the sake of argument) that the being and nature of the material world is independent of God's creative will. And it loses its interest as soon as we abandon this highly unorthodox supposition.

Of course, as Kant sees, we might try to use the phenomena of nature to argue that the existence of matter itself is contingent on God. But, he points out, to do this

Would require us to be able to prove that the things of the world would be unsuitable to this sort of order and harmony in accordance with universal laws unless they were, in their substance itself, the product of a highest wisdom. But this would require grounds of proof wholly different from those supplied by the analogy with human art. . . . If we want to prove the contingency of matter itself, we have to resort to a transcendental argument; but that is just what we set out to avoid.⁶⁷

Here, then, Kant once again sounds his main theme: Physicotheology is incapable of establishing the existence of a God who resembles the orthodox one unless it calls to its aid precisely those rationalistic and metaphysical arguments for which it expresses such contempt. Moreover, Kant seems to be on firmer ground here than he was before. The empiricist theologican might plausibly maintain that the concept of an *ens realissimum*

67. *Critique of Pure Reason*, A 627/B 655.

or ontologically perfect being is merely an invention of philosophers, with little or no relevance to orthodox Judaeo-Christian faiths, but he will have more difficulty saying this about God as the creator on whom all things depend, the "maker of heaven and earth, and of all things visible and invisible."

The Use and Abuse of Theism in Natural Science

Kant was firmly convinced of the heuristic value of the theistic hypothesis for the study of nature. But he also thought that physicotheology is capable of obstructing and misleading scientific inquiry if it is misapplied, or if its role in empirical investigation is misconstrued. As early as the *Beweisgrund* essay, Kant criticized what he called the "usual method of physicotheology" for appealing to the divine will as a principle of explanation in ways which are both unwarranted and detrimental to the progress of science.[68] In the *Critique of Pure Reason*, Kant describes two "errors" which may result if the idea of God is misused. The first, which he calls *ignava ratio* or "lazy reason," is the error of trying to explain natural phenomena by direct appeal to the divine will, rather than investigating the details of the arrangement through which a natural purpose comes about. This is an error because the whole point of the theistic hypothesis in science is to keep us watchful for such arrangements; the "lazy reasoner" uses it as an excuse for doing just the opposite.[69]

The second error Kant calls *perversa ratio* or *hysteron proteron rationis*; it occurs when we use theism not as a guide for discovering purposes in nature, but as an occasion for imposing them "dictatorially" on it. The "perversion" Kant means is apparently one of ignoring altogether the purposive self-organization actually found in nature, and insisting that something or other serves a divine purpose solely on the basis of capricious and "anthropomorphic" fantasies about what God's will is.[70]

Kant thinks these errors will be avoided if we are careful to employ the idea of an intelligent author of nature only "regula-

68. *Gesammelte Schriften*, 2:116ff.
69. *Gesammelte Schriften*, 28, 2, 2, p. 997; *Lectures on Philosophical Theology*, p. 29.
70. *Critique of Pure Reason*, A 689/B 717.

tively" and never "constitutively." To use this idea only "regulatively" is to view all unity and combination in the world "as if
it collectively arose from a single all-encompassing being as supreme and all-sufficient cause," without "positing," "hypo-
statizing," or "assuming absolutely" an object of this idea.[71]
Thus Kant seems to be recommending to natural science that it
use the idea of God merely as a heuristic device: that it look in
nature for the order and purposive combination it might expect
if there were a God, but not take what it finds as real evidence
for such a hypothesis.

It is easy enough to see how such a "regulative" use of the
idea of God would avoid the two errors against which he warns
us. For if we do not permit ourselves to employ the purposiveness in nature as evidence in favor of the theistic hypothesis,
then we cannot use this hypothesis to provide any genuine
explanation of the phenomena of organization: the lazy reasoner
is therefore deprived of the easy chair in which he was inclined
to rest content with his dogmatic explanations. Still less are we
likely to indulge in any speculations about the purposes of
God's will which have no empirical basis. For we are not supposed to let ourselves think that even the natural purposes we
do find are genuine signs of God's will.

On the other hand, there is no reason, as far as I can see, why
a natural scientist who uses the idea of God "constitutively"
might not also avoid these errors. If we believe that natural purposes are real signs of God's will at work, this does not necessarily make us any less interested in the intricate details of the
purposive arrangement, or any more likely to ignore them. Still
less does it *commit* us to ignoring the details, or to formulating
groundless dogmas about the divine will. Kant's desire to
eschew the two errors thus falls short of making it necessary for
him to employ the idea of God only "regulatively" and not
"constitutively." At least, Kant's prescription is more extreme
than the disease requires.

The heuristic value of theism is supposed to lie in the fact
that if we look at the world theistically, we are led to expect

71. *Critique of Pure Reason*, A 686/B 714, A 685/B 713, A 693/B 721, A 698/B,
726.

unity and combination in nature, and this expectation helps us
to discover cases of such unity which we might otherwise have
overlooked. But then why doesn't the organization we find in
nature count as evidence in favor of the hypothesis which led us
to expect it? Kant's answer seems to be that theism does not
lead us to expect any *particular sort* of order, combination, or
organization, but only provides us with the best way of making
intelligible to ourselves an expectation of contingent order in
general. Thus it serves only to *maximize* our expectation of harmony and order in nature, and not to suggest any particular sort
of order or purpose rather than any other:

> The presupposition of a supreme intelligence as the sole cause of the
> world whole . . . can always benefit reason and never harm it. For . . .
> by following this path we can make a multitude of discoveries. If we
> retain this presupposition only as a regulative principle, even error
> cannot harm us. For nothing more can follow from it than that where
> we expect a teleological connection (*nexus finalis*) we meet with only a
> mechanical or physical one (*nexus effectivus*). In such a case, we merely
> fail to discover a unity, but we do not damage the unity of reason in its
> empirical employment.[72]

It seems to me that Kant is not right about this. The hypothesis of an intelligent cause would suggest to us that sort of order
which might especially appeal to a *conscious* being; and the hypothesis of a morally good author of nature suggests an order
which would tend to further moral purposes. By contrast, the
Spinozist hypothesis would suggest an order which is cold,
amoral, indifferent to the concerns of conscious beings. The
whole point of Kantian moral faith, after all, depends on the
assumption that the belief in an intelligent and morally perfect
author of nature leads us to have different hopes and expecta-
tions about the moral orientation of the world's order than atheistic beliefs would. If a Spinozist or materialist hypothesis about
the cause of order in the world led us to no different expecta-
tions in this regard, then there would be no reason at all for the
moral man to be a theist rather than a Spinozist or materialist.

Theism, therefore, has heuristic value for natural science inso-

---

72. *Critique of Pure Reason*, A 687f/B 715f.

far as the order waiting to be discovered in nature is in fact the
sort of order theism suggests, rather than some other kind. But
then the discovery of this particular sort of order tends to confirm not only the heuristic value of theism but also its truth as
an explanatory hypothesis about the way things really are. On
the other hand, the discovery of different kinds of order tends
to disconfirm theism both "regulatively" and "constitutively."
The gratuitous beauty of nature's products, for instance, might
be taken to count as evidence in favor of theism and against
Spinozism; whereas the seemingly arbitrary way in which the
suffering of conscious beings has been built into nature's order
might tend to count in the opposite direction. Perhaps the evidence is mixed or hard to interpret, but that does not prevent it
from being genuine evidence in favor of rival hypotheses.

Kant may be relying at this point on his view that theism is
the only real candidate as an explanation of order in the natural
world. He may mean to claim that theism leads us to expect no
special sort of order in nature because none of the other hypotheses we might use to explain any kind of purposive order turn
out to be able to do so satisfactorily. In that case, however, we
may make the same point here which we made earlier with
regard to Kant's disposition of the possibility proof. If theism is
the only distinctly conceivable explanation for natural order of
any kind, then the discovery of any sort of order at all would
surely count as evidence in its favor. At the same time, however,
the *heuristic* value of theism in such a case would be minimal. It
can't tell us very much about what to look for, since it tells us
only to expect the maximum of unity and organization in nature. Unless terms like "unity" and "organization" already give
us a clue as to what we are looking for, the theistic hypothesis
will be no guide at all. But if such terms by themselves do suffice
to tell us what to look for, then the theistic hypothesis will not
be needed for this purpose.

Kant is therefore faced with a dilemma: Either (1) the theistic
hypothesis suggests some particular kind of order, different in
certain respects from its atheistic alternatives; or (2) it suggests
only order in general, and not order of any particular kind. If we
accept the first option, then the theistic hypothesis has heuristic

value for science only if the actual order in nature tends to be of the particular sort suggested by theism. But in that case, the order found in nature counts as genuine empirical evidence in favor of theism, and against its atheistic rivals. Theism is justified "constitutively," and not merely "regulatively." On the other hand, if we embrace the second option, the heuristic value of theism is going to be minimal. The "regulative" employment of the hypothesis will be of little use to us. However we look at the matter, it is hard to sustain Kant's conclusion that the idea of God should be employed as a heuristic device in the empirical study of nature, but the theistic hypothesis should not be treated as an object of empirical confirmation or disconfirmation.

Concluding Remarks

The usual view of Kant's rational theology is that its negative side is much more successful than its positive side. Kant's criticisms of the received proofs for God's existence has frequently been lauded as an epoch-making, even a "world-destroying" achievement. On the other hand, his positive account of the rational idea of God has often been dismissed as a tedious rehash of Wolffian dogmatic metaphysics, and inconsistent with Kant's critical principles.

In the foregoing essay, I have been arguing toward a different conclusion. I have tried to show that Kant's argument for the rational inevitability of the idea of an *ens realissimum* is an original and well thought out one, making use of conceptions which belong to a long metaphysical tradition. The argument is an insightful development of hints found in the writings of Leibniz, and is a significant improvement over the simpler parallel argument for the same conclusion formulated by Descartes and taken over by Wolff. The argument, moreover, is entirely compatible with the principles of the critical philosophy, and accomplishes an important part of Kant's task in the Dialectic of the *Critique of Pure Reason*. If, despite this, the argument strikes us as tortuous and artificial, this is largely because we lack sympathy with the set of metaphysical presuppositions on which it rests: with the rationalist conception of God, the traditional ontology, and the Leibnizian conceptions of individuality and possibility. It is no doubt true that Kant's critical philosophy served historically to initiate an intellectual movement through which this metaphysics was eventually overthrown. But an accurate account of the critical philosophy itself must take into account Kant's own sympathies with rationalist metaphysics, as well as the extent to which he managed to render its principles compatible with his critical views and to incorporate them into his philosophy.

Much less successful, I have argued, is Kant's attack on the traditional proofs for God's existence. In his desire to systematize his criticism of the theistic proofs, Kant organized it around his attack on the ontological proof, claiming that the basic deficiency of the cosmological and physicotheological proofs was their covert reliance on it. But this claim, as we have seen, was simply not convincingly made out by Kant for either proof. He failed to show that the cosmological proof depends on the ontological, or even that acceptance of the former proof requires acceptance of the latter. His treatment of the physicotheological proof was even less persuasive on this point. The most he showed was that this proof cannot by itself establish the existence of an *ens realissimum* or prove that the material world depends for its being and fundamental nature on an intelligent creator. Kant made no case at all that physicotheology itself is dependent on or committed to either of the transcendental proofs.

Probably the most serious drawback of Kant's strategy, however, is that it prevented him from following up several more promising lines of criticism of the cosmological and physicotheological proofs. Kant's treatment of the third and fourth antinomies, for example, contained materials which might possibly have been developed into a convincing refutation of the cosmological inference from contingent existence to necessary existence. But owing to his strategy, Kant let this inference, like the physicotheological inference from purposive order to a designing intelligence, pass by virtually unquestioned.

Neither is Kant's criticism of the ontological proof made out as well as it should be. Kant does advance a coherent (and widely accepted) thesis about existence and predication which, if correct, would dispose of the ontological proof. But this thesis is not self-evident, and it has sometimes been rejected even by opponents of the proof. Kant's only real argument for the thesis, moreover, is a conspicuously sophistical one. Here again, much better ways of criticizing the proof were open to him. For example, he might well have attacked Descartes' argument more effectively if he had based his criticism on a critical rejection of some of its rationalist epistemological presuppositions.

It seems to me, therefore, that the Kantian critique of the traditional theistic proofs is on the whole unsuccessful. No serious defender of any of the proofs need give them up as a result of Kant's criticisms. Kant did not even at this point make particularly good use of the critical tools he provided himself earlier in the *Critique*: in every case stronger reasons for rejecting the proofs were available to him. If, as a matter of intellectual history, Kant's attack succeeded in bringing those proofs into disrepute, then we must conclude that it did not do so on its philosophical merits.

One reason, I think, why the positive side of Kant's thought on the subject of rational theology has been inadequately appreciated is that its presentation in the *Critique of Pure Reason* is both very narrow in scope and dreadfully obscure in expression. In every respect, the *Lectures on Philosophical Theology* exhibit this side of Kant's thinking in a richer, and more intelligible form. These lectures, however, until a few years ago, were not readily available, and the scholarly attention devoted to their contents is still virtually nothing compared to the appalling bulk of the literature on most other parts of the Kantian corpus. No doubt a certain misplaced purism persuades some scholars that they may, or even must, ignore texts which do not come from Kant's own hand, but are based on lecture notes taken by others. The *Lectures*, however, do deserve study. They show clearly Kant's great sympathy with the scholastic-rationalist theology found in the texts of Eberhard and Baumgarten. In their detailed criticisms and revisions of the views found in these texts, the *Lectures* also show, I believe, that the traditional theology was to a large extent compatible with Kant's critical philosophy. They indicate that Kant appreciated (as do many contemporary philosophers) the inherent conceptual interest of questions about the divine attributes and the relation of the world to an eternal, extramundane creator, even granting a theoretical agnosticism about the existence of such a being. And of course they also show Kant working to give substance to his rational moral faith, by developing his own critical version of the scholastic-rationalist conception of God.

It is true that at the present time this brand of theology does not command a wide intellectual respect. Naturally those who reject theism in any form may be expected to find unpersuasive the pretensions of rational theology to the status of a metaphysical science, just as Kant did. But even unbelieving philosophers often appreciate the intricate conceptual problems raised by rational theology, whose discussion by important historical philosophers frequently bears directly on problems of importance even to the least religious-minded. What is ironic is that many theologians and religious thinkers in recent times have been even more contemptuous of rational theology than these unbelievers. Orienting themselves to scripture, to ecclesiastical tradition, or to one or another form of nonrational religious encounter, they have often been even more anxious than the atheists to repudiate the conception of God derived from scholastic and rationalist metaphysics. Many modern theologians, and by no means only "modernist" ones, try to do without any philosophically articulated concept of God whatever. Others, like Paul Tillich, attempt to formulate a new conception out of materials provided by post-Kantian German idealism. Process theology is another attempt to bring theology "up to date" by appealing to less traditional metaphysical views.

Kant himself was in many ways a "modernist" and even an "existentialist" theologian. As I have argued elsewhere,[1] his moral religion was fundamentally a religion of hope and personal commitment, a religion whose source was the "existential" predicament of finite human nature. His attitude toward churches and scriptures, as exhibited in *Religion within the Limits of Reason* and the *Conflict of the Faculties*, was anything but a traditionalist one. On one point, however, Kant's theology re-

1. *Kant's Moral Religion*, especially pp. 1–10, 153–187, 249–254.

mained quite conservative. It drew its object of moral faith from an idea generated by theoretical reason, the idea of an *ens realissimum*. And it developed this idea, as the *Lectures* show us, very much along the lines of traditional scholastic and rationalist theology.

On this point, I think, Kant's instincts were basically sound. If religious faith involves an existential commitment of the believer's whole being, that commitment cannot fail to express itself in a rational, theoretical account of the content of its belief. No amount of emphasis on the "existential" or "experiential" side of religion, and no reliance on scriptural revelation or dependence on the community of the faithful, can take away this responsibility, which arises from the believer's own rational nature. If, as in Kant's case, religious faith takes some supernatural absolute being as its object, then it is impossible for the believer to avoid the issues raised by traditional theology. The conception of God worked out by this tradition is perhaps beset with philosophical difficulties, and it is not easy to reconcile it with certain essential aspects of any modern world outlook. But none of the more recent attempts to articulate the concept of the absolute or the divine has managed to give as rich, precise, philosophically sophisticated, or rationally credible an account of it. To face up squarely to the problems of the tradition, as Kant did, remains by far the most straightforward and intellectually honest way for a modern theologian to discharge his philosophical responsibilities.

Index

Library of Congress Cataloging in Publication Data
(For library cataloging purposes only)

Wood, Allen W
  Kant's rational theology.

  Includes index.
  1. Kant, Immanuel, 1724–1804. 2. Religion—Philosophy. I. Title.
B2799.R4W66   200′.1   78-58059
ISBN 0-8014-1200-5